Halee Gray Scott is a committed Christ-follower whose passion is that all humans—especially women—live out their influence. She models a life that dares mighty things and inspires others to take up the challenge for themselves.

—Elisa Morgan, speaker, author, President Emerita, MOPS International

Halee Gray Scott's timely book moves women beyond the gender debate zone to deal with the practical challenges women face in the often uncharted territory of ministry leadership. We need to get on with the work God is calling us to do and to call other women to join us. *Dare Mighty Things* is full of practical wisdom to help women leaders avoid the potholes in the road ahead that slow us down unnecessarily and cause avoidable casualties. This book is an important resource I will be recommending to women leaders I know.

—Carolyn Custis James, author, *Half the Church*

Reading *Dare Mighty Things*, I felt that Halee Scott knew me intimately and urgently spoke the truth I needed to hear. I've spent thirty years as a marketplace Christian leader, and now I serve as a nonprofit ministry leader. I've never heard anyone articulate so vividly the challenges we face as leaders and how God would have us stand in the face of them. This book activated new resolve and passion for the mighty things God is calling me to do. It will do the same for you!

—Tami Heim, President and CEO, Christian Leadership Alliance

Occasionally a book comes along with the power to inspire significant change. *Dare Mighty Things* qualifies, and I couldn't put it down. Halee tackles the key leadership challenges Christian women face today with researched insight, candor, and optimism. Over and over, I marveled at the wisdom of her beautiful young voice, calling women out of the shadows to experience the joy of leading for the Lord. I wish I could whisper these truths in the ear of every woman who wonders why she is here and how God wants her to spend her life. *Dare Mighty Things* provides a map that could revolutionize her world and rejuvenate the church.

—Dr. Sue Edwards, Associate Professor of Educational Ministries
and Leadership, Dallas Theological Seminary

Dr. Halee Scott's *Dare Mighty Things* is a much-needed book for all Christian women, especially women who sense a call to ministry work. Halee acknowledges and articulates obstacles of female leadership within the church, but she doesn't let us wallow there. She challenges us to redefine the meaning of leadership, to live with grit, to work hard, and to dare too much rather than too little. *Dare Mighty Things* invites women into the high call of living all out for Jesus and his kingdom work.

—Dr. Jackie Roese, President, The Marcella Project

Finally someone has filled the need for a smart, savvy, and balanced resource for women in leadership. Women who often find themselves emerging alone are now part of the honest conversation Halee Gray Scott brings. As a pastor who has worked with women for more than a decade, I have been waiting years for a resource like this. Thank you, Halee!

—Rev. Tracey Bianchi, Pastor for Worship and Women,
Christ Church of Oak Brook

Halee Gray Scott dares women to discover how their lives matter, how they are gifted and called by God, and how they are needed as leaders today. She does not pit Christian complementarians and egalitarians against one another. Instead she finds points of collaboration: how women can be leaders, how spiritual gifts are not engendered, how all Christians— including women—have a responsibility to exercise and steward their giftedness, and how churches have a responsibility to ensure that women are able to exercise their giftedness in freedom. Scott's book is soundly biblical and theological, critical and creative, inspiring and practically applicable.

—Don Thorsen, Professor of Theology, Azusa Pacific University

I once heard a speaker say that many Christian women fall into the trap of trying either to "lead like a man" or "be nice like a girl." Halee Gray Scott offers an alternative. She calls for women to live as women in Christ Jesus. From the table of contents to the very last page, this book is inspiring and instructive, especially to those women who can feel a sense of destiny inside them. If you're female and you want to live for God, then dare mighty things, because God created women to show his greatness.

—Sarah Sumner, author, *Men and Women in the Church: Building Consensus on Christian Leadership*

DARE MIGHTY THINGS

MAPPING *the* CHALLENGES *of* LEADERSHIP

for CHRISTIAN WOMEN

HALEE GRAY SCOTT

ZONDERVAN

Dare Mighty Things
Copyright © 2014 by Halee Gray Scott

This title is also available as a Zondervan ebook. Visit www.zondervan.com/ebooks.

Requests for information should be addressed to:

Zondervan, *Grand Rapids, Michigan 49530*

Library of Congress Cataloging-in-Publication Data

Scott, Halee Gray, 1978–
 Dare mighty things : mapping the challenges of leadership for Christian women / Halee
Gray Scott.
  pages cm
 Includes bibliographical references.
 ISBN 978-0-310-51444-2 (softcover)
 1. Christian women—Religious life. 2. Leadership in women. 3. Leadership—Religious
aspects—Christianity. 4. Women in church work. 5. Christian leadership. I. Title.
BV4527.S284 2014
253.082—dc23   2013036966

Cover design: Michelle Lenger
Cover photography: © Veer, Shutterstock
Interior design: David Conn

Printed in the United States of America

14 15 16 17 18 19 20 21 22 /DCI/ 20 19 18 17 16 15 14 13 12 11 10 9 8 7 6 5 4 3 2 1

For my daughters:
Viv, spirited as a high wind,
and
Ellie, bright as the morning
God has used you both, already, in a mighty way
to heal places in me long devastated.
I'm so, so happy
to be your mama.

CONTENTS

ACKNOWLEDGMENTS

Thank you, Amy. Your wit and courage were the muse for all this, all those years ago. I'm so proud of all you have accomplished.

Thank you, colleagues at Hermeneutics, in Redbud Writers Guild, and beyond. Your voices and wisdom illuminated my way.

Thank you, Katya. Your incisive, brilliant work made this book a better one.

Thank you, Sarah. Your faith and relationship with God have been a tremendous inspiration to me.

Thank you, Myrna, for seeing the end before it came to pass. A girl could never ask for a better soul sister.

Thank you to the women who took the time to share their stories with me. This is your book, your story, and I'm so amazed at what the Lord is accomplishing through your lives.

Thank you, KK. Your kindness, generosity, and encouragement helped bring this book into being.

Thank you, Nanny. You've been so steady, so sure, all my life. I hope someday I can be half the mother and grandmother you have always been.

Thank you, Paul. None of this would be possible without your love, support, and encouragement. I'm so blessed to be your wife.

INTRODUCTION

Far better it is to dare mighty things, to win glorious triumphs,
even though checkered by failure, than to take rank with those
poor spirits who neither enjoy much nor suffer much, because
they live in the gray twilight that knows not victory nor defeat.

—Theodore Roosevelt, "The Strenuous Life"

This is what you need to know about Christian women. We are ladling hot soup into empty bowls, building food pantries and vocational schools among the urban poor. We are demonstrating what it really means to be a neighbor, giving up posh lifestyles to live among distressed immigrant families. We are carrying out the very kind of life the rich young ruler could not,[1] leaving lucrative careers to found or serve in organizations that provide aid and sustenance to foreign countries. We are taking the long road in the same direction, dedicating decades of our lives to the faithful, quiet shepherding of a single congregation. We are pouring medicine on open wounds, braving inhospitable environments to bring God's healing Word to hurting, secular places.

If we are not doing (yet), we are dreaming. As children, we see the world as wide, brimming with possibility. In our pure, unadulterated adoration for God, we do not fully understand the limitations and challenges we will face in a life of service to God. As young women, we slip our feet into shoes that do not yet fit, trying out ministry in various forms—volunteering at vacation Bible school, taking short-term mission trips with our families or youth groups. As college women, we are chess masters, sorting out the various pieces of our lives and searching for a strategy to make our lives matter. As seminarians, now older and with great sobriety, we take risks and put feet to our girlhood dreams. As single women, we try to prove our value to God's kingdom even though we do not have husbands or families; as married women, we try to prove our value to God's kingdom even though we do.

We are motivated not by power or money but by a desire to make our lives count. At the end of things, we want to know that our breath was not in vain, that our days were not swallowed up by the mighty tide of human history. As Tolkien put it, we want "to do what is in us for the succour of those years wherein we are set, uprooting the evil in the fields that we know, so that those who live after may have clean earth to till."[2] We want our children and the children of our neighbors the world over to set their feet in a greener, more spacious place. God has given us eyes to see, hearts to love, hands to tend, and with gratitude we want to offer these hearts, these hands, back to God for all he has accomplished for us, in us.

And yet the church has failed Christian women because it has failed to cast a comprehensive vision of what God can accomplish in and through the life of a woman. So in the midst of all our doing and dreaming, our strength is blunted. Our roads often end at an impasse or a gorge too wide to traverse. Without a social connection to other women, we feel isolated and alone. Without mentors, we recreate the wheel, starting at square one over and over again with no guide to help us. Without advocates who believe in our gifts and abilities, we have no one to invest in us. Faced with these difficulties, along with many others, we are tempted to give up, to think we misunderstood our calling. It is easy to dismiss our childhood dreams as nothing more than fairy tales.

Perhaps even more gravely, the church has failed Christian women twice because it has not articulated the virtue of a strenuous life and it has not equipped us to live (or desire) such a life. In the context of a culture that prioritizes ease and luxury as keys to a happy life, it is all too easy for women to lose heart and believe the challenges are too great to summit. As the French say, *Ça ne vaut pas la peine*—"it is not worth the pain."

Through my research, I have spoken with female Christian leaders for the last seven years about their experiences, trying to nail down the top obstacles that prevent Christian women from thriving in leadership. This book is the result of those conversations. In this book, I hope to provide a roadmap for women to follow by outlining the ten most common challenges women face in ministry leadership. By telling the stories of Christian women, I aim to provide a vision of what God can accomplish through women's lives. But neither of these will prove fruitful without a firm understanding of the virtue and the beauty of the strenuous life.

President Theodore Roosevelt understood the virtue of the strenuous life. Theodore "Teddy" Roosevelt was not expected to live to adulthood. As a child, he suffered from a stomach disease called cholera morbus and asthma attacks so severe his family feared he would not live to his fifth birthday. He was so sickly that his family homeschooled him. On Sundays, his father swooped him off to the clean air of the country. But Teddy's parents struggled under the burden of his asthma. His mother writes, "Teedie ... seems hardly to have three or four days complete exemption [from the illness] and keeps us constantly uneasy and on the stretch."[3]

Doctors warned him to live a quiet life, choose a sedentary occupation, and avoid strenuous activity. After consulting multiple doctors, his father built Teddy a gymnasium on their property and told him, "Theodore, you have the mind, but you have not the body, and without the help of the body, the mind cannot go as far as it should. I am giving you the tools, but it is up to you to make your body."[4] Without hesitation, Teddy responded, "I will make my body!" In that very moment, Roosevelt became a fierce advocate for what he called "the strenuous life," a life that did not shrink from danger or challenges but embraced them in order to conquer them.

That small, sickly boy went on to become a successful boxer at Harvard, as well as to dabble in wrestling, jiujitsu, and judo. But sport was not the only area in which he excelled. He became a New York State assemblyman, governor of New York, police commissioner of New York City, US civil service commissioner, assistant secretary of the navy, colonel of the Rough Riders, vice president, and the youngest president ever to take office. He read at least a book a day and wrote more than thirty of his own. He increased the national forests by forty million acres and established five national parks and sixteen national monuments (including the Grand Canyon). He won a Nobel Peace Prize for his role as a peacemaker in the Russo-Japanese War. He was a devoted husband and loving father to six children.

On April 10, 1899, Roosevelt, then the governor of New York, delivered a speech titled "The Strenuous Life" at the Hamilton Club in Chicago, a prestigious political fraternity for the wealthy. Chicago had always been a city with two faces. Its population exploded from 500,000 people in 1880 to 1.7 million in 1900. The city swallowed up whole the smaller rural communities just outside its border, luring small-town farmers and factory workers to the industrial plants popping up in the city. Buildings, too, sprang up all over like dandelion weeds.

For the working poor, Chicago was *The Jungle*,[5] a place of grinding poverty, dangerous and deplorable working conditions, low pay, and job insecurity. But for the wealthy, for those who built colossal fortunes off the backs of the Reconstruction and the Industrial

Revolution, Chicago was a premier city of the world in which to build a cultured life of leisure and ease. Roosevelt saw the impulse toward a comfortable life growing among the wealthy, and it concerned him, for he believed that genuine happiness, "the good life," was found not in a life of comfort, free of struggle, but rather in a life that saw challenges as opportunities for personal growth. "A life of slothful ease, a life of that peace which springs merely from lack either of desire or of power to strive after great things, is as little worthy of a nation as of an individual. We admire the man who embodies victorious effort; the man who never wrongs his neighbor, who is prompt to help a friend, but who has those virile qualities necessary to win in the stern strife of actual life. It is hard to fail, but it is worse never to have tried to succeed.... Far better it is to dare mighty things, to win glorious triumphs, even though checkered by failure, than to take rank with those poor spirits who neither enjoy much nor suffer much, because they live in the gray twilight that knows not victory nor defeat."[6]

Roosevelt understood what it means to struggle, strive, and survive, and he sought to remind these men in "the greatest city of the West" of their heritage as descendants of people who did not shrink from doing the right thing—such as engaging in a civil war that ultimately procured freedom for four million slaves—even though they would suffer great losses. Roosevelt believed that the highest form of success was not a life of ease but a life that welcomed danger, toil, and hardship in order to better someone else's life.

Roosevelt knew intuitively what researchers are beginning to discover: the key to "the good life"—the kind of life that brings the most fulfillment and happiness—lies in taking on challenges and doing things that are risky. It seems paradoxical that the kinds of activities that threaten our immediate happiness would result in our long-term happiness and well-being, but that is exactly what researchers are finding.[7] Happy people are continually compelled to do hard things.

When we take on challenges, we have to grapple with a degree of uncertainty. We risk failure. We risk losing. We risk getting hurt. But whether we fail or succeed, doing risky things expands our vision of what is possible, builds our character, and equips us with the skills, the confidence, and the attributes we need to navigate with aplomb the difficult situations life inevitably throws our way. Like lifting weights or walking uphill, resistance makes you stronger. The moment you stop facing challenges or obstacles is the moment you stop growing.

Roosevelt knew the men of his day were capable of achieving extraordinary things; all he needed to do was call them back to what the good life really is. His concerns are perhaps even more valid today than they were a hundred years ago. In Western culture, we are diverted and aimless. We have more leisure time than our ancestors, but we are not sure what we ought to do with it, so we often spend it on purposeless activities like television, movies, gaming, and the internet. We want more for less effort, and we have been duped into thinking that this is the good life. Yet we are still depressed, anxious, and lost. Is this the good life? Some think that still more leisure and less work will finally alleviate these problems, but how could it? Our problem is not that we dare too much; it is that we dare far too little.

Sadly, the church has not articulated a meaningful corrective to the gospel of leisure and ease, and in many cases, we have only endorsed it. We have changed our music, changed our messages, and traded our pews for movie-theater seats, all in an effort to appeal to people who prioritize entertainment and ease. And yet it is still not winning people to the church, and in many cases, it is turning even the most faithful away from regular church attendance. There have been no Roosevelts to inspire us, to help us question our priorities, to tell us that the good life—real happiness, real contentment—lies in daring mighty things by allowing God to accomplish great things through us.

People are not moved to action by appeals to what even they know are the lesser aspects of their nature; people are moved by that which appeals to the highest aspects of their character. People are moved when you tell them they are gifted, they are needed, and that their lives matter. People are moved when you make a place for them to let their giftedness shine. People are moved when you appeal to that part of them that culture has silenced, that place long dormant that desires to achieve impossible, unbelievable things.

There is no one for whom this is truer than Christian women. Christian women have been shamed into a corner. Many have bought the lie that they are the second sex—that they do not matter and that they are not gifted, at least not in the ways that matter most. They got the message that they need to limit their horizons, temper their ambitions. They are leaving. Research shows not only that there are fewer women in church but also that there are fewer women going to seminary. Women's advancement in leadership has altogether stalled, right along with the wage gap. Women, especially Millennial women, see this lack of progress and wonder whether leadership is even worth it. So they look for the good life elsewhere. *Ça ne vaut pas la peine.*

Christian women, it is not enough for me to simply tell you the stories of Christian women who are daring mighty things and outline the challenges you will face, so let me tell you this:

- *Your life matters.* Like Roosevelt said, we can learn from *our* ancestors, from Christian women who dared mighty things and brought about massive cultural reform. It was not too long ago that women in the nineteenth century, women with far more limitations than we have today, worked to abolish slavery, alcoholism, poverty, illiteracy. They created legislation to prevent women from being sexually exploited by men, built homes to keep them safe, and provided aid to immigrants.
- *You are gifted and called.* The Lord can do more than you can possibly imagine through your life.
- *You are needed.* The same problems that confronted the women of the nineteenth century confront us today. Women are still

exploited by men. Slavery is not abolished for all. Fifteen million children go to bed hungry every night in America alone. We can find the good life by daring mighty things, by overcoming our personal challenges in order to make a good life for others.

God is working through Christian women. The first challenge for most Christian women? Believing you are a leader at all. Believing you have gifts. Believing that God wants to use your life as a force for good. Not every woman is called to be a pastor, a minister, or a CEO of a nonprofit. Some women are called to lead in other ways — leading an at-home Bible study, starting a food pantry at their church — but these women are leaders too, and their contributions have been minimized for far too long.

Sometimes the mightiest thing you can do is to do that which seems very small: dare to dream big dreams. Dare to believe that you can make a difference. Dare to believe that overcoming obstacles and facing challenges is worthwhile. In the following chapters, I discuss the key obstacles for Christian women. Women have overcome them before; all you have to do is dare to believe that you can too. That is where you start.

CHAPTER 1
TERRA INCOGNITA

CHARTING NEW TERRITORY *for* CHRISTIAN WOMEN

To lose track of our stories is to be profoundly impoverished not only humanly but also spiritually.

—Frederick Buechner, *Telling Secrets*

For as long as I can remember, I have been drawn to lonely places, to places long forgotten or places undiscovered. The badlands of the Texas Panhandle are the beginning of the American West. Most people, from Spanish explorers in the sixteenth century to modern-day travelers of US Route 66, thought of the Panhandle, an area sparsely vegetated with cacti, crooked honey mesquite, and juniper trees, as a land you just passed through.

Our family passed through it every year at Christmas as we made our way from one set of grandparents to the other. Through the back window of my parents' Grand Marquis, I would peer out at the arid landscape riddled with canyons filled with tall grasses, plums, and hackberries and long for another kind of life. I daydreamed about being a cowgirl exploring the Palo Duro Canyons on a palomino quarter horse.

Years later, while going to grad school, my husband and I lived in a parsonage on the edge of the San Gabriel Mountains in Glendora, California. Los Angeles County is the most populous county in the nation, but you would never know it from the top of Colby Trail. Despite a demanding schedule working three jobs in addition to full-time PhD coursework, I still headed out my back door three or four times a week to explore miles of often-isolated trails.

Still even more years later, I chiseled out my dissertation on the edge of another range of mountains — the Colorado Rockies. Local lore is filled with harrowing tales of expedition and discovery, but the story that made the biggest impression on me was the story of Lewis and Clark, who passed through the Rocky Mountains near Lincoln, Montana.

When Meriwether Lewis and William Clark embarked on their legendary expedition in May of 1804, President Thomas Jefferson commissioned them to find a direct water route across the continent to facilitate commerce, and to discover and document the resources in the newly acquired Louisiana Purchase. In May 1804, the land stretching from North Dakota westward to the Pacific was *terra incognita* — unknown territory.

The story of Lewis and Clark underscored something I had believed from those early days sitting in the back seat of my parents' car: it is not that lonely places have no stories; it is that their stories are still waiting to be told. I guess it is this same impulse to find the untold stories that first stoked my interest in female Christian leaders. In the twenty-first century, we are inclined to think that there are no unknown territories, no frontiers left uncharted. Yet when we seek to explore and explain the experiences of female Christian leaders, we are embarking, like Lewis and Clark, on a journey into *terra incognita*.

Though there are women leading in almost every area of Christian ministry, they are not that visible. We know very little about their experiences and the challenges they face. Because of this, Christian women are often either sidelined or their efforts are altogether derailed.

TALES FROM THE SIDELINES

Samantha[1] was thirteen months old when her parents divorced. Her father was never around or involved in her life, and her mother worked seventy hours a week to support Samantha and her three siblings. For most of her life, Samantha felt that she had to figure things out on her own. I met Samantha during her sophomore year at Azusa Pacific University (APU), where I worked as an adjunct professor and reference librarian.

When you are nineteen years old and fresh out of your parents' home, it's easy to get caught up in the carefree college days and put off making big decisions like which major to pursue or what career God may be calling you to. But Samantha did not waste any time. She double-majored in political science and history and worked part-time at the library to pay the amount of her tuition that was not covered by her scholarship.

Samantha was thoughtful, disciplined, and desperate to make a difference in the world, but she was often frustrated by the lack of thoughtful resources for Christian women. "I feel called to do something in ministry," she told me, "but I have no idea how to get there. When I go to a bookstore to look for guidance on how to develop as a female Christian leader, I don't find any meaningful Christian resources to help me. I don't know any female Christian leaders in the organizations I'd like to serve in."

Helen was a fellow professor at APU. One spring morning we talked softly in the library, savoring the lull in activity that always comes midsemester. The semester had been launched, lesson plans were written, and final exams were in the distant future. We talked about theology, about our students, about our stage fright when giving lectures. But most of all, we talked about our futures. Both of us had achieved significant accomplishments at a fairly early age: she had been the recipient of the only full scholarship that Fuller Theological Seminary offers MDiv students, and I was a published writer wrapping up the final semester of coursework for my PhD.

Both of us had been encouraged by mentors throughout our academic careers, about our potential for contributing to the academic community, about charting new territories for female Christian scholars. And we loved academia and the life of the mind. We never thought—in all our years of learning and studying and teaching and writing—that anything, even our gender, would stand in our way. Both the feminists and our fathers had taught us that we could accomplish anything we wanted to, that the world was ours for the taking, that we were limited only by the things we chose not to do.

But on that March morning, we secretly admitted that we did not feel the academic world was all we wanted out of life. We did not just want to be Christian scholars and professors; we wanted to be mothers. And we wondered how on earth two such demanding, seemingly opposing spheres of life could ever be reconciled and how we could participate fully, incarnationally, in both worlds. I remember the tension building as we spoke, our minds scrambling for answers to what we thought were new questions. "The problem," I said, "is that we have no maps." At the time, neither one of us had appropriate role models to guide us; our mentors were either men or women with no children.

Sally was one of the best in the business. She knew how to get things done and how to build relationships with potential donors. For years, she had been a happy stay-at-home mom to her three kids, until her husband lost his job and the financial house of cards came tumbling down. Sally got an entry-level job at a local nonprofit Christian ministry, and soon her quick mind for business catapulted her through the ranks of the organization.

When I met Sally, she was a senior vice president at a nonprofit Christian ministry, the only female vice president the company had ever had. For the most part, Sally loved her job, her staff, and her relationships with donors, but she struggled in her relationship to the president and the other vice presidents. As is the case with most organizations, a great deal of knowledge and information was shared during informal meetings, such as at lunch or during an afternoon of golf, but because she was female, she was often excluded from these informal get-togethers.

As a result, Sally found it impossible to get decisions made in her division. She cared about the quality of her work and the ministry her organization did, and she wanted to find out how to circumvent this issue. "I'm the only woman VP I know," Sally told me. "How do other women manage this?"

The stories of Samantha, Helen, and Sally illustrate the felt need that Christian women have — to respond well to God's calling on their lives by exercising and stewarding their giftedness. But they also point to a certain degree of isolation and confusion about how to do so. Though there are women serving as leaders in most Christian organizations, the stories of these women have been lost.

LOST WOMEN IN CHRISTIAN MINISTRY

It is not just contemporary stories of women that have been "lost." A quick review of published history texts reveals that women have disappeared from the annals of church history as well. In their book, *Daughters of the Church*, Ruth Tucker and Walter Liefeld note that the role of women in religion "down through the ages has been flagrantly neglected, despite longstanding appeals to historians to do otherwise."[2] Tucker and Liefeld wrote *Daughters of the Church*, which traces the contributions of Christian women throughout church history, because they believed "separate volumes on women in the church are the only way of telling their story."[3]

Tucker and Liefeld dive deeply into ancient texts to uncover and tell the stories of women in church history. But how do you tell the stories of Christian women serving in ministry today? One of the best and most efficient ways we have for uncovering truth—for telling the stories—in our time is research, which is the systematic investigation into a particular subject. Like the detective work of Sherlock Holmes or the best investigative reporting, research helps us to explore, explain, and describe. From research we are able to understand reality and take action accordingly.

For example, throughout most of history, if you went to the doctor for a headache, he most likely would have tried to alleviate the pain by removing small amounts of your blood using vacuum cups, lancets, or leeches. Bloodletting was the most common medical practice throughout the world. It was such a common practice that the Roman encyclopedist Aulus Cornelius Celsus wrote that "to let blood by incising a vein is no novelty; what is novel is that there should be scarcely any malady in which blood may not be let."[4] Luckily, the research of a young scientist named Louis Pasteur, by changing what was known, changed the practice of medicine. Bloodletting fell into disfavor with the emergence of the germ theory of disease, which postulates that illness is caused by bacteria, not by an imbalance in bodily humors.

Research tells us *what is*, and from there we are able to make informed decisions and take appropriate actions in a given situation. It inoculates us against isolation and the futility of recreating the wheel or repeating the same mistakes because it shows us that others have already been where we are. For female Christian leaders serving in ministry, the trouble is that there is hardly any research that speaks directly to their situation. This is one reason why Samantha found it so difficult to find thoughtful Christian resources to help her grow as a Christian leader.

In contrast, there is so much secular research about female leaders that one can hardly get to the end of it. Since the early 1970s, at the height of the feminist movement, researchers the world over have investigated whatever question or concern one could possibly have regarding women and leadership. We know the efficacy of female leaders in a variety of contexts—from business to politics to law to the military to secular nonprofit humanitarian organizations. We know, roughly, the number of female leaders in a given context, how female leaders compare with men, the styles of leadership that women adopt, how to expand opportunities for female leaders, the common challenges they face, and how these challenges are overcome.

We do not have the same information about *Christian* female leaders because Christian female leaders have rarely been subjects of serious study. Even in a lightning-fast information age, female Christian leaders have escaped our notice largely because we do not have enough of the right people asking enough of the right questions. The Association of Theological Schools (ATS) is an organizing body of 253 seminaries and other graduate schools of theology. Thirty-five percent of these graduate schools are related to an undergraduate college or university. Though women earn more than half of both master's degrees and PhDs in the US overall, women in ATS-accredited schools comprise only 34 percent of the student body and 22 percent of the faculty. Fewer women in these schools leads to fewer women examining Christian leadership issues at the doctoral or faculty levels.

Of course, there are ways to learn about the stories of female Christian leaders apart from research, such as through networking, media, social media, and think-tank groups like the Barna Group, but the issue of female leaders is greatly complicated by the often contentious theological disagreement between complementarians and egalitarians on the nature of women's leadership.

A HOUSE DIVIDED

The bulk of the conversation about female Christian leaders is centered firmly on the theological debate between complementarians and egalitarians. The arguments of complementarians can be summarized in three statements. First, complementarians believe that while women are equal to men in value and status before God, men and women are designed for a complementary relationship, one enhancing the role of the other. According to John Piper and Wayne Grudem, men are to serve as the "head" or leader in the home and in the church, while women are to serve as helpers in submissive assistance to men. Piper and Grudem further state, "Biblical headship for the husband is the divine calling to take primary responsibility for Christlike, servant-leadership, protection, and provision in the home. Biblical submission for the wife is the divine calling to honor and affirm her husband's leadership and help carry it through according to her gifts."[5]

Second, the fall disrupted God's original created design, introducing a host of issues within the relationship between the man and the woman, including a desire on the part of the woman to "conquer or rule over, or else an urge or impulse ... to oppose her husband, an impulse to act against him, which would ultimately result in man ruling over her not as one who leads among equals, but rather one who rules by virtue of power and strength, and sometimes even rules harshly and selfishly."[6]

Third, through redemption in Christ, gender roles between the man and woman in marriage and in the church are properly restored to what God created them to be and differentiated from one another. Man is instructed to exercise male headship and woman is instructed to graciously submit to the authority of her husband.[7]

The complementarian argument for differentiation in gender roles is generally centered around six passages of Scripture, including Genesis 1–3; 1 Corinthians 11:1–16; 1 Corinthians 14:33–36; 1 Timothy 2:8 15; Ephesians 5:21 33; and 1 Peter 3:7.

In contrast to the positions articulated by complementarians, egalitarians believe that women are both equal to men in value and status before God, as well as functionally equal to men. Women should have the same opportunities for leadership as do men, without prohibitions barring them from official positions such as senior pastor.

The logical flow of the arguments by egalitarians can, like the complementarian arguments, be summarized in three statements.

First, egalitarians believe that it is logically inconsistent to say that men and women are equal in *essence* or *being*, but not in *function*. Rebecca Merrill Groothuis writes, "The question of whether a being/function distinction is logically applicable to a defense of gender hierarchy is a crucial one, because this distinction is foundational to every traditionalist argument today. When traditionalists affirm in theory the essential, spiritual equality of women and men, but feel no obligation to advocate the full practical ramifications of such equality, they invoke as their rationale the notion that women's subordination is only 'functional' and has nothing to do with her essential being."[8] Both men and women are created in God's image (ontological equality), and both are given the task of stewarding the rest of creation (functional equality).

Second, egalitarians claim that the fall disrupted the equality between men and women. Men and women were given dominion (i.e., stewardship) over the earth, and when Adam and Eve transgressed and used that dominion inappropriately, the punishment involved a disruption in the relationship between the man and the woman. Consequently, "her sociability was mixed with the problem of social enmeshment, which continues to hamper the proper exercise of her dominion in the world at large," while the man's legitimate dominion "became laced with the problems of domination—which has been interfering with his relationships—to God, to the creation, and to other people, including women, ever since."[9]

Third, egalitarians maintain that through the life and teachings of Jesus, as well as his atoning work through the cross, the effects of the fall have been reversed and equality has been restored. Into the patriarchal society that had been inappropriately dominated by men throughout history came a rabbi with a surprising view toward women—who openly taught women, encouraged their learning and growth, whose teachings included feminine perspectives at times, who "allowed women to be the first witnesses of his resurrection and a woman to proclaim that event to his male disciples."[10]

The argument for ontological and functional equality typically hinges on six key verses: Genesis 1:26–27; Genesis 2:18; Genesis

2:22–24; Galatians 3:28; 1 Corinthians 11:11–12; and 1 Corinthians 12:7–11.

The subject of women in ministerial leadership positions, even in the evangelical church, is a hotly contested debate with little hope of resolution in sight. Both sides of the argument have well-developed reasoning and sound positions for their views. Both are committed to the authority of Scripture. Both sides are equally committed to the evangelical tradition; both sides draw compelling arguments from the biblical text. Both are revising historical church tradition, a tradition that for the most part viewed women as ontologically inferior to men.

Yet both sides have been injured by the arguments of the other because the argument takes place in a larger context that includes the abusive male chauvinism that has dominated most cultures and also the radical feminism that denied the authority of Scripture and sought to redefine and reinterpret the Scriptures in light of the new agenda. This context makes it difficult for one side to hear the other.

Theologian Henri Blocher, in the volume *Women, Ministry, and the Gospel*, comments, "Many complementarians believe that the inevitable logic of the egalitarian view leads directly to radical feminism, and they oppose it, not only because of what it teaches about the role of women in the home and in the church, but also because of what its ultimate trajectory might be."[11] Likewise, egalitarians view the complementarian positions as nothing more than a modified version of male chauvinism, "an effort to suppress the God-given gifts based not really on biblical truths but on a cultural captivity that borders on ... idolatry."[12]

For real dialogue and reconciliation to take place, these fears must be fully understood and recognized by both sides.

THE LAST THING ON JESUS' MIND

In the hours approaching his agony, Jesus prayed for his followers. "The hour has come," he says to the Father (John 17:1)—the hour of his appointment with the cross, a time of separation, betrayal, suffering, and crucifixion. Jesus prays for himself, that he be glorified. He prays for his disciples to be protected from the evil one and that they be sanctified (17:15, 17). He prays for you and for me, for future believers, that we will be one, united, so that the world will know that God loves us and sent Jesus to us, for us (17:21).

Jesus prayed for us. In the hours approaching his hours of agony, we *really were* on his mind. And his concern was that we would be one, united, a reflection of the Most Holy Trinity. The stress on the unity of believers is clear, for five times in thirteen verses he mentions "one" or "unity," the Greek word *hen*, meaning "in opposition to a division into parts, and in ethical matters to dissensions, to be united most closely in will, spirit."[13]

Regardless of whether you interpret Jesus' prayer for unity as an imperative for us to follow or a petition for the Father to work on our behalf, one has to agree that church unity was foremost on his mind in the moments leading up to the cross. Dr. Gilbert Bilezikian comments, "According to that prayer, the most convincing proof of the gospel is the perceptible oneness of [Jesus'] followers."[14]

The theme of unity was also important to the apostle Paul. The Corinthian church was a divided church with a lot of problems — serious problems, we would say, including incest and doctrinal issues like the denial of the future resurrection. But of all their problems, the one Paul addresses first and foremost is the problem of church division. He begins his letter to them with an exhortation to be united: "I appeal to you, brothers, by the name of our Lord Jesus Christ, that all of you agree, and that there be no divisions among you, but that you be united in the same mind and the same judgment. For it has been reported to me by Chloe's people that there is quarreling among you, my brothers" (1 Cor. 1:10–11). No less than twenty times are we urged in the New Testament to be architects of unity. "I ... implore you," begs the apostle Paul, "to walk in a manner worthy of the calling with which you have been called, with all humility and gentleness, with patience, showing tolerance for one another in love, being diligent to preserve the unity of the Spirit in the bond of peace" (Eph. 4:1–3 NASB).

God is not glorified and people are not blessed by divisions and contentious debates between Christians. "In our day," writes Bilezikian, "whenever the church is ineffective and its witness remains unproductive, the first questions that must be raised are whether the church functions as authentic and whether it lives out the reality of its oneness."[15] And there are plenty of divisions or "tribes" among evangelicals. There are the conservatives and liberals, the Republicans and Democrats, the traditional worshipers and the contemporary worshipers, the Methodists and the Baptists and the nondenominationals, and, of course, the complementarians and egalitarians.

Being unified does not mean a lack of diversity or unique perspectives, any more than there is a lack of diversity among the Father, Son, and Holy Spirit, but it does mean that we demonstrate tolerance and respect for one another by working together for God's purposes and refusing to malign those who differ from us. There is room in evangelicalism to maintain both the particular views regarding female leaders and the commonality to which we are called, just as there is both unity and diversity in the Holy Trinity.

THE WAY FORWARD

The battle lines between complementarians and egalitarians have long been drawn. Nothing new has been said, and it appears that we all have arrived at a stalemate. Nobody is winning, least of all the church, for the theological debate gobbles up so much of the conversation about women that it is difficult to move forward to talk about something else, such as how to support and encourage female leaders. Please do not misunderstand me. The theological conversation about female leaders is *an important* conversation, but it's not *the only* conversation we should be having.

"But wait!" one might say. "Complementarians don't believe that women can be leaders." This is not true. Whether women can exercise leadership or be people of influence has never been the question. The focal question is the extent of their leadership. Complementarians restrict women from formal leadership positions in the church and from leading men, but they are leaders—of other women and of children—nonetheless.

The failure to move forward in our conversation about female leaders to discuss how we can support, encourage, and equip them hurts the church because "half the church" is woefully underprepared for the ministry to which they are called by the nature of their individual giftedness. Women hurt because they are not able to exercise their gifts. The world hurts because far too many Christian women expect far too little of themselves, and their small expectations are no match for the world's great need.

In her book *Half the Church*, Carolyn Custis James laments the "anorexic spiritual diet" of so many Christian women and the "small visions" they hold about God's purposes for themselves. "When half the church holds back—whether by choice or because we have no choice—everybody loses and our mission suffers setbacks."[16]

Thankfully, there is a far more excellent way. Complementarians and egalitarians have far more in common than many think. Not only do they have a common enemy and a common task to seek the kingdom of God to defeat the work of that enemy; they agree on the following points:

1. *Women can be leaders.* The opportunities of women serving in complementarian contexts are restricted in the sense that they are not able to lead or teach men, but even in these contexts, there is great opportunity for women to lead other women and children. Further, Piper and Grudem allow for women to "be leaders" by visiting the sick, counseling both men and women, and leading Christian education programs, missionary programs, and other evangelistic efforts.

2. *The spiritual gifts are not gendered.* The genesis of leadership is grounded in the spiritual gifts, which are freely given by God

without respect to gender, race, or social class. In Joel 2:28–29 we read that the Spirit is universally poured out on "all flesh," and because of this, both our "sons and daughters will prophesy." Miroslav Volf comments, "*All* God's people are gifted and called to various tasks by the Spirit," and this understanding "provides us with biblical illustrations of human work: intellectual (e.g., teaching) or manual (e.g., crafts) work, *poiesis* (e.g., arts and crafts) or *praxis* (e.g., ruling)."[17] For Volf, all human work, including leadership, is made possible through the Spirit of God working in the person.

Unfortunately, this is one of the great misunderstandings in the church today. I've spoken with so many women over the years who express confusion over how the spiritual gifts are relevant in their own lives when it seems that so many opportunities to exercise those gifts are limited. When these women hear sermons on spiritual gifts, they often feel as though the pastor is addressing men alone, since so many of the spiritual gifts involve activities that are off-limits for them. "How can I do that," they wonder, "when I don't have 'the same plumbing' as my father, brother, or husband?"

3. *All Christians, including women, have a responsibility to exercise and steward their giftedness.* First Peter 4:10–11 reads, "As each one has received a special gift, employ it in serving one another as good stewards of the manifold grace of God.... Whoever serves is to do so as one who is serving by the strength which God supplies; so that in all things God may be glorified" (NASB). Whatever their spiritual gift may be, both men and women are to be faithful in using it to strengthen others' faith. Women are not free to ignore, neglect, squander, or bury their gifts out of fear. Sometimes doing nothing at all is as wrong as overtly committing a sin. In the parable of the talents, Jesus describes inaction as "wicked" (Matt. 25:26). Both complementarians and egalitarians agree it is important for women to be faithful in stewarding their spiritual gifts,

even when, perhaps *especially when*, their spiritual gifts lead to places of leadership.

4. *Communities of faith have a responsibility to ensure that women are able to exercise their giftedness in freedom.* If a church does not utilize the giftedness of their members, they are in contradiction with the Scriptures. If Christians are responsible to steward their gifts, communities of faith—for which the spiritual gifts exist (Eph. 4)—have a responsibility to ensure that *all* of their members have the opportunity to use their gifts for the building up of the body of Christ. In a discussion of Titus 2:4–5, Piper and Grudem note that "it is indeed unfortunate that an overemphasis on trained male leadership fulfilling every aspect of ministry in the local church has excluded 'women elders of women' ... the pastor who fails to draw on the Biblical resource of qualified older women ... is not only risking the effectiveness of his ministry but also operating in clear contradiction to Scripture."[18]

With these four things held in common between complementarians and egalitarians, we can begin to move forward on the issue of Christian female leaders by recovering the stories of those who serve and identifying the challenges that lie ahead. We do not have to agree on the finer points of women's ordination or the extent of the spheres of women's influence to agree that both men and women and communities of faith have a responsibility to wisely steward the giftedness in their midst.

CONCLUSION

Lewis and Clark never did find a direct water route across the continent, but they produced the first accurate maps of the area and demonstrated that overland passage to the Pacific was possible. In a similar way, I hope that this book serves as a map to help Christian women navigate key leadership challenges and that it demonstrates that a life of leadership—a life of influence—is possible for Christian women.

Part of stewarding our giftedness and the giftedness of others is understanding the limitations and challenges of what we are trying to do. The way to leadership is often lonely for Christian women. I often hear women comment, "I'm the only one." Yet it's not that there are no other female Christian leaders; it's that their stories have yet to be told.

In this book, we begin by clearing up the mystique surrounding what leadership is by discussing what leaders actually do. What makes a person a leader? Next, we show how Christian women are serving God as leaders around the globe in Christian education, churches, and parachurch organizations. Finally, we discuss successful strategies for navigating ten challenges that Christian women will face on their journey to places of influence.

CHAPTER 2
WHAT IS LEADERSHIP?

WHAT LEADERS DO

The Master [Leader] doesn't talk, he acts. When his work is done, the people say, "Amazing! We did it—all by ourselves!"

—Lao Tzu, *Tao Te Ching*

She was a Sunday school teacher. Henrietta Mears was born in Fargo, North Dakota, in 1890, the youngest of seven children. Her vision was so poor that doctors told her parents that she would be completely blind by the time she was thirty. Convinced that God had a purpose for her life, she memorized large portions of Scripture and, against her doctor's advice, enrolled at the University of Minnesota. For several years after college, she worked as a teacher in schools throughout Minnesota, teaching chemistry and drama.

In 1928 she accepted an incredible opportunity to become the Christian Education Director at Hollywood First United Presbyterian Church in Hollywood, California. When she arrived, it was already a healthy program with more than 450 students, but within two years of her arrival, it grew to more than 4,000. She did not like the curriculum the church offered, so she wrote her own. Eventually, other churches wanted her curriculum, so she founded Gospel Light Publications in order to meet that need.

Mrs. Mears, or "Teacher" as her students called her, firmly believed in the value of Christian camping, so she bought Forest Home, then a private resort in the San Bernardino Mountains, for $30,000 — less than a tenth of the estimated value. "There is no magic in small plans," she said. "When I consider my ministry, I think of the world. Anything less than that would not be worthy of Christ nor his will for my life."[1]

Through her ministry at Hollywood First United Presbyterian Church and her curriculum, Henrietta Mears was the "spiritual grandmother" to a few of those who founded and led the most prominent ministries of the twentieth century, including Campus Crusade for Christ, the Billy Graham Evangelical Association, Youth for Christ, the Navigators, and Young Life.[2] But Henrietta Mears was not a president or a pastor. She was a Sunday school teacher. Sometimes the best leaders are hidden in the most inconspicuous places. Sometimes the best leaders are the most inconspicuous people. In this chapter, we'll take a look at what leadership means, what the Bible says about leadership, and why women often do not see themselves as leaders.

WHAT DO LEADERS DO?

What comes to mind when you hear the word *leader*? Do you think of a specific president, like George Washington, Abraham Lincoln, or John F. Kennedy? Do you think of politicians in general, the CEO of a company, a military leader, a biblical figure like Moses or Deborah, or the pastor of your church?

When we think of leadership in general, our minds tend to lean toward the greatest (or worst) examples of leadership. By doing this, we inadvertently overlook the common ways people lead every single day: the volunteer coordinator of the church's prayer team, the director of the local rescue mission, the Dutch baker downtown who employs a staff of twenty to provide artisan breads for the community, the shift supervisor at the local McDonald's, the coach of the fourth-grade boys' baseball team, the entrepreneur of a small ministry devoted to sheltering sex-trafficked victims, the fitness instructor who coaches people toward a healthier lifestyle, the teacher leading third-grade students on a nature walk, the mother teaching her children important life skills.

As political analyst Dee Dee Myers wrote, "I am endlessly fascinated that playing football is considered a training ground for leadership, but raising children isn't."[3] As we try to discern what the heart of leadership is, we need to keep in mind all the ways that people lead, both big and small.

Defining leadership is about as easy as nailing jelly to the wall. The term is slippery for three big reasons. First, *leadership* is difficult to define because the term has lost some of its meaning because of what Marilyn Chandler McEntyre calls "habitual verbal promiscuity."[4] Like the words *dynamic, wonderful, awesome, great,* and *amazing, leadership* has lost precision because of misuse and overuse.

For example, we often use *leader* synonymously with *outperformer.* When Wall Street lists the day's stock volume leaders, they mean the most actively traded stock for that day. We call athletes like Aaron Rodgers, Babe Ruth, and Jackie Joyner-Kersee the "leaders" in their respective sports. The widespread use and misuse of the terms *leadership* and *leader* distorts our perception of what real leadership means. When a word is used to mean everything, it fails to mean *something.*

The second reason leadership is so hard to conceptualize is because it has been approached in different ways over time. Just in the last century, there have been at least ten very different ways of approaching leadership, from the "Great Man" approach of the early twentieth century to the "authentic leader" approach of the early twenty-first century:

APPROACH	THE IDEAL LEADER	FOCUS	YEARS
Great Man	Ideal leaders are "great men" with innate, fixed traits	Leader	Early–mid 20th century
Skills	Ideal leaders have certain skills	Leader	1955–present
Style	Ideal leaders have certain styles	Leader	1948–1960s
Situational	Ideal leadership depends on situation	Situation	1969–present
Contingency	Ideal leaders match their style to the situation	Leader and situation	1960s–present
Path-Goal	Ideal leaders motivate followers to accomplish the leader's goals	Followers	1990–2000s
Servant	Ideal leaders are first servants	Followers	1970s–present
Transformational	Ideal leaders transform followers	Followers	1970s–present
Authentic	Ideal leaders are relationally transparent; honest leadership	Followers	September 11, 2001–present

Basically, what this chart tells us is that in one hundred years, we have moved from looking for leaders like Winston Churchill to looking for leaders like Oprah. What changes in each of these approaches is the understanding of what makes a good leader. Is it certain traits a person is born with? A certain skill set or style? Is good leadership focused on the leader or the follower? Our desires for what we want in a leader are not fixed. Approaches change because people change. The times change.

During World War II, a military conflict that claimed the lives of more than 60 million people, we needed a "Great Man" leader like Winston Churchill, a man with the chutzpah and tenacity to stare down monsters like Hitler and Mussolini. It was not until after the war that the "Great Man" theory of leadership began to be challenged. People started thinking that leaders were made, not born.

After the September 11, 2001, terrorist attacks, Americans started looking for a new kind of leader. We had already moved from the "control and command" style of leadership that characterized some of history's greatest leaders — like George Patton and Margaret Thatcher — toward a type of leadership that focused on people's needs rather than the objectives of the leader. This transformational leadership style focused on modeling the way, enabling others to act, inspiring vision, and encouraging the hearts of followers.

But after 9/11, we wanted more than just a transformational leader. We want someone *authentic*, someone trustworthy to guide us, and the financial horrors of Enron, the Bernie Madoff Ponzi scheme, and the global financial crisis have only deepened that desire.

With so many different ways of understanding what ideal leadership is, it is easy to see why we have not arrived at a consensus on what it means to be a leader.

The final reason leadership is difficult to define is because leadership, like love, beauty, or wisdom, is a broad concept. As Warren Bennis notes in *On Becoming a Leader*, "Leadership is like beauty: it's hard to define but you know it when you see it."[5] There are as many definitions of leadership as there are people to define it.[6] In a survey of scholarly literature written from 1900 to 1990, leadership scholar Joseph Rost discovered 221 distinctive definitions of leadership in

587 books and journal articles.[7] Here's how a handful of leadership experts and thinkers have defined it:

- "The only definition of a leader is someone who has followers" (Peter Drucker).[8]
- "Leadership is influence — nothing more, nothing less" (John Maxwell).[9]
- "Leadership is a process whereby an individual influences a group of individuals to achieve a common goal" (Peter Northouse).[10]
- "Leadership is that which leaves the world a better and different place, that is you lead people in new directions, to solve problems and make new things happen. You stretch people to achieve things they didn't think were possible" (Rosabeth Moss Kanter).[11]
- "Effective and transformative leadership is one that derives from the values inherent in the architecture, ideology, and symbolism of motherhood ... mothering the nation tends to convey the idea of diffused and restorative power" (Filomina Chioma Steady).[12]
- "A leader is anyone with a vision who understands and voices the needs of the community, develops a constituency, and facilitates the involvement and development of others to bring about social change" (Martha Zurita).[13]

The first three definitions were written by the most-often-cited leadership experts, all of whom happen to be Western, white, and male. These particular men have made important contributions to the field of leadership and they have the loudest voices in the discussion of leadership around the globe. But arriving at a more robust, ecumenical understanding of leadership — one that reaches beyond these definitions to take into account the voices of women and minorities — requires deeper and more deliberate excavation.

The common thread woven throughout these definitions is the concept of influence, which is the ability to have an effect on another person's character, behavior, or actions. Leadership expert Peter Northouse's definition above — "Leadership is a process whereby an individual influences a group of individuals to achieve a common goal"[14] — encompasses all levels of leadership, from great to small. It includes the larger-than-life leaders like Billy Graham, who led more than 400 crusades in 185 different countries, and it includes the millions of unsung heroes who lead in small but significant ways every single day.

THE SHEPHERD LEADER: THE BIBLE AND LEADERSHIP

In their book *Spiritual Leadership*, Henry and Richard Blackaby raise the important question, "Is Christian leadership the same thing as secular leadership?"[15] It is a necessary question because along with the rise of megachurches came the tendency to adopt a corporate business model for the intention of running a successful church. Churches began to emphasize "seeker-friendly" services and rely on marketing techniques to make the church seem more appealing to "outsiders." As church attendance grew with these business techniques, the role of the pastor naturally began to be viewed as akin to the role of a CEO.

Though the CEO model of the pastorate has come under harsh criticism in recent years, the definitions of Christian leadership still have the same tenor of secular definitions of leadership. Consider these examples:

- "A Christian leader is someone who is called by God to lead; leads with and through Christlike character; and demonstrates the functional competencies that permit effective leadership to take place" (George Barna).[16]
- "Leadership is a process of influence. Anytime you seek to influence the thinking, behavior, or development of people in their personal lives, you are taking on the role of a leader" (Ken Blanchard and Phil Hodges).[17]

- "The central task of leadership is influencing God's people towards God's purposes" (Robert Clinton).[18]
- "Leadership is influence; Christian leadership is Christlike influence"[19] (Greg Ogden and Daniel Meyer).
- "Leadership is moving people on to God's agenda"[20] (Henry Blackaby and Richard Blackaby).

Functional. Competencies. Influence. Development. Agenda. While these definitions are consistent with biblical principles, they are still heavily reliant on secular language and thinking about the practice of leadership. This is not to say that all of what the secular market says about leadership is bad; indeed, a quick perusal of the bookshelves containing contemporary leadership principles seems to read like a compendium of ancient spiritual wisdom: *Jesus, CEO*; *Servant Leadership*; *The Transforming Leader*; *The Spirit of Leadership*; and *The Tao of Leadership*.

While I agree that leadership is "influence" and I applaud the recent developments in contemporary culture that move leadership thinking toward more holistic, people-centered models, most of the definitions proposed by both secular and Christian sources still ring hollow to me. In adopting the corporate and political language of leadership, the church forfeited a treasure: the timeless model of the shepherd as leader.

In the ancient world, shepherds were people of low regard, yet they were used as the image of effective leadership throughout ancient cultures. In the Scriptures, the shepherd motif is used from beginning to end. In Jeremiah 3:15, the Lord promises, "And I will give you shepherds after my own heart, who will feed you with knowledge and understanding." In Acts 20:28, the apostle Paul advises the elders of the church in Ephesus, "Be on guard for yourselves and for all the flock, among which the Holy Spirit has made you overseers, to shepherd the church of God which He purchased with His own blood" (NASB).

Though we need to be reacquainted with the tasks of the shepherd, the metaphor of "shepherd as leader" remains as valid today as it did in the time of Moses or Hammurabi. In his book *Shepherds After My Own Heart*, Timothy Laniak identifies four duties of the shepherd: presence, protection, provision, and guidance.

The first duty of the shepherd was to be present, and not just physically present but attentively, mindfully present to the flock under his care. As Proverbs 27:23 advises, "Know well the condition of your flocks, and give attention to your herds." The responsible shepherd knows "every member of their flock in terms of their birth circumstances, history of health, eating habits, and other idiosyncrasies."[21] This intimate, personal knowledge of the flock ensures that the shepherd knows the best way to guide them through difficult terrain and environments without driving them too hard (Gen. 33:13).

The second duty of the shepherd was to protect the flock. The wilderness was rife with menacing threats to the flock, from natural predators such as wolves, bears, and lions to human threats such as thieves. The task of the shepherd was to be constantly vigilant in protecting the flock from these enemies. In the beloved Psalm 23:4, we read of the emotional and psychological results of the shepherd's protection: "Even though I walk through the valley of the shadow of death [the land of many dangers], I will fear no evil, for you are with me."

The third duty of the shepherd was to provide food, water, and rest. A healthy flock was dependent upon a right balance of these elements. With an intimate knowledge of each member of the flock, the environment, and the weather, the shepherd was able to ensure that his flock was well provided for. "The LORD is my shepherd," the psalm reads,

> I shall not want.
> He makes me lie down in green pastures.
> He leads me beside still waters.
> He restores my soul.

> —Psalm 23:1–3

The fourth duty of the shepherd was to guide the flock. "Sheep are typically led from in front," notes Laniak, "but they are occasionally driven from behind according to the shepherd's plan."[22] Again, the intimate knowledge of the flock—whether they were young, old, pregnant, or injured—allowed the shepherd to guide his flock with compassion according to his plan.

The shepherd motif is so strong throughout Scripture that the Greek word for shepherd, *poimaino* or *poiman*, is often translated as *pastor* in the New Testament. The shepherd model of leadership gives texture to the leadership process. It is not so much that the secular definition (and the corresponding biblical definitions) of leadership as "a process whereby an individual influences a group of individuals to achieve a common goal" is wrong so much as it is incomplete.

Biblical leadership is not just about influencing others toward a goal, for the task of the shepherd-leader is much more comprehensive. It involves knowing the flock, their limitations and their needs, knowing the goal or destination, and knowing how to get them there. "Good shepherding," writes Laniak, "is expressed by decisions and behaviors that benefit the 'flock' at great personal cost. It calls for the benevolent use of authority ... some situations require militant protection and discipline, others beckon for gentle nurture."[23]

WHY WOMEN DO NOT SEE THEMSELVES AS LEADERS

The secular definition of leadership as "a process of influence" and the four tasks of the shepherd-leader (presence, protection, provision, and guidance) are not particularly masculine in nature, yet many still view these as essentially masculine tasks, associating "leadership" and "shepherding" as exclusively male domains. As a result, women, especially Christian women, fail to see themselves as leaders. In a chapter on exploring the nature of leadership, it is important to address issues that may prevent women from viewing themselves as leaders.

Growing up in Minneapolis, Debbie Jonnes never thought of herself as a leader. She was the last person picked for the soccer team and the last to take a lead role in anything. Always a shy, introverted person without a great deal of confidence, she shied away from opportunities to be in front of others. "I think I always compared myself to others. I thought leadership had more to do with an outgoing personality, charisma, or a captivating presence with great vision—which wasn't me."

Though Debbie "didn't have a strong sense of confidence" in her ability to lead, as she felt that some of the messages she had received in life pointed to her deficiencies rather than her competencies, others eventually did have confidence in her, and they placed her in roles with greater and greater responsibility. With the support of other leaders who challenged her and encouraged her to take on more leadership roles, Debbie gained more confidence in her leadership gifts. Today, Debbie is the director of the Women's Center at New York City's historic Bowery Mission. Along with a team of ten women, Debbie ministers to women in crisis, whether they are homeless, unemployed, struggling with addictions, or victims of domestic violence. In addition to being available 24/7 for these women, Debbie provides general oversight for the program and the staff and takes a role in fundraising for the organization.

There are several reasons why many women, like Debbie, fail to recognize themselves as leaders, including a lack of encouragement, the tendency to "shrink to fit" others' expectations, and shame.

LACK OF ENCOURAGEMENT

I do not think James meant to be unkind. I was sitting in the antiques mall my dad and stepmom own in downtown Mineola, Texas, mindlessly surfing the internet behind the counter when James, a longtime family friend, approached me. I was still bleary-eyed from months of writing my dissertation, the final piece of my PhD. "Halee, I'm so proud of what you accomplished," James said. I smiled at him in gratitude, and he leaned in closer and whispered,

"Ya know, nobody 'round here thought you'd come ta much, but I knew better."

At a loss for words, I simply blinked at him. What should you say in a moment like that? I did not know, so I said nothing. Besides, he was probably right. The real surprise would have been discovering someone actually believed way back then that I would manage to pull myself together enough to do anything meaningful with my life. I was a latchkey kid with a difficult home life, and I was constantly in trouble. I received "licks" almost every single year from kindergarten through sixth grade. The tongue-in-cheek caption in the Quitman Independent School District's annual yearbook sums it up well. Under a photo of me flashing an impish grin, it reads, "Third-grader Halee Gray: 90 percent angel, 10 percent devil."

I realized over time that no matter what your home life is like and no matter how much encouragement you do or do not receive, at the end of the day, you still have this: the wondrous gift of being able to forge your own path and your own life. And I decided I did not want my life to end badly. I wanted it to count. But I fought discouragement and self-doubt every day. For the most part, I felt invisible, and if I had any gifts at all, I did not know what they were and neither, it seemed, did anybody else.

This would be nothing more than an unfortunate anecdote if my story were just an anomaly or an outlier, but it is not. Thousands of women have this same story, if not much worse. No one has actually stopped to really *see* them, to acknowledge a germ of giftedness lying dormant within them. No one has taken the time to nurture that giftedness into full-bodied life. Some women, like Debbie and I, did not receive encouragement growing up; others may have received it early on but failed to get it in early adulthood when they were chiseling out a career path because political or organizational structures barred women from participating in leadership.

Elizabeth had to go outside the Christian community to discover and cultivate her leadership gifts. She'd been serving as a missionary in France alongside her husband for many years before she realized that being a missionary was not the best use of her gifts. It was back before the Iron Curtain fell, and her husband was researching new ways to get the gospel into the Soviet Union and the Middle East, but the organization they served with at the time did not recognize the gifts and talents she could offer the ministry. "It was a big disappointment to find out they really didn't want me," Elizabeth said. "They just wanted my husband."

Elizabeth wanted to set an example for her children of what a Christian woman looked like beyond using her gifts as a missionary wife, so she plugged into a local acting club that cultivated an interest in the arts, an interest that eventually led her to a position as an assistant at an art gallery. In that role, she learned she had a mind for business and corporate fundraising. Today, Elizabeth travels the world for the same organization her husband worked for in France, leading courses for local church leaders, teaching them about fundraising, sustainability, and how to depend on local generosity rather than funds from the West.

Elizabeth's story is an example of how organizations, both churches and Christian nonprofits, fail to recognize the leadership gifts of Christian women in the West, but Christian women in other parts of the world also face political and societal barriers to leadership. Dr. Annie George, a professor at Faith Theological Seminary in Adoor, India, advises her female students to be sure they are called to ministry because ministry is difficult for women in India. She points out, "Women may not be able to use all of their talents because of the political structures in India. The way society is set up prevents women from leading in ways they may be gifted for."

The failure to encourage the giftedness and leadership abilities of women is born in the poverty of our expectations. Like Nathanael, who doubted that anything good could come from Nazareth, we fail to encourage the giftedness of women because we do not expect them to have certain leadership gifts. Whether they be the English parlor maid, the mischievous latchkey kid, the troubled teen, the missionary's wife, the young woman from the Dharavi slum in

Mumbai or the Kibera slum in Nairobi, we do not see their leadership gifts because *we do not expect them to have any.*

Our expectations govern what we see. Inattentional blindness, also known as perceptual blindness, is "the striking failure to notice a fully visible but unexpected object when attention is otherwise engaged."[24] In one of the most widely known studies conducted to observe this phenomenon, research psychologists Daniel Simons and Christopher Chabris asked participants to watch a video in which two teams, one in black shirts and one in white shirts, are passing a ball. Researchers ask participants to count the number of times the team in the white shirts passes the ball. Halfway through the video, a gorilla walks in the midst of the players and beats his chest before walking away.

At the end of the video, participants are asked how many times the ball was passed. Then researchers ask, "But did you see the gorilla?" Incredibly, more than half the time, participants miss the gorilla entirely.[25]

We think we see everything as it is in reality, but really, what we see is largely dependent upon our own expectations. When it comes to identifying and encouraging female leaders, we cannot encourage when we cannot see and we cannot see what we do not expect.

Encouragement changes things. American essayist Ralph Waldo Emerson noted, "Our chief want is someone who will inspire us to be what we know we could be." The word *encourage* comes from the Old French word *encoragier*, which means "make strong; hearten." It's derived from the word *en*, "to put into," and *courage*, "heart; innermost feelings," and *heart* is metaphorically associated with the concept of inner strength. Thus, to encourage someone literally means "to pour strength into" them.

It is possible, I suppose, for women to become leaders without the encouragement of others, but not likely. Most of us have those days when we lack the inner strength to put one foot in front of the other, let alone the strength to identify our own giftedness and persevere through the various challenges in the path to leadership.

SHRINK TO FIT

Sarah has a first-rate mind, but she has learned how to keep it under wraps—especially on dates. As a master's degree student at Talbot School of Theology, she meets mostly young men who are preparing for careers in Christian academia or ministry. In the past three years, it has been rare for someone from her classes to ask her out on a date, and when someone does, she sometimes feels as though she has to hide who she really is.

Rather than engage them in a philosophical or theological discussion, she sticks to more superficial topics. She will tell them she teaches, but she will not say she teaches at the collegiate level. She will not tell them she makes straight As, plays the piano, that she was a five time All-American, that she won the state championship for hurdle events her senior year of high school, or that she plans to pursue a PhD. Men usually react to Sarah in one of three ways: they ignore her, verbalize their insecurity, or try to compete with her.

Shawna and her husband, Tim, are co-lead pastors of Bakersfield First Church of the Nazarene in Bakersfield, California. Shawna is good at leading meetings and providing direction to groups of people, but it is only in her husband's absence that she takes the lead in church meetings. Whether it is a meeting with the board or the worship team, she handles them capably, but when Tim is present, she automatically draws back without thinking much about it. "We didn't even realize this was happening until he stepped into an event that I had been leading and there was suddenly tension when I didn't step back and let him lead," she said. "We had to laugh about it when we finally talked because we both consider ourselves to be advocates for women's voices and leadership."

Both Sarah and Shawna hide their giftedness from others. Sarah did so in an overt way in order to protect the feelings of the young men she dated, while Shawna did so in a more subconscious manner by simply taking the back seat at meetings when her husband was present. Hiding giftedness or abilities is not a problem specific to Christian women or even women in the twenty-first century. In the late eighteenth century, Jane Austen incisively wrote, "A woman, especially, if she have the misfortune of knowing anything, should conceal it as well as she can."

Women learn early to hide their abilities. In a study of gifted adolescents, researchers found that 65 percent of girls consistently hide their talents.[26] Girls also seem to learn that certain intellectual and leadership gifts are not appreciated and are perhaps even negative. When parents of boys and girls with similar aptitudes for leadership were asked if they thought their children had leadership abilities, parents (usually mothers) would write lengthy explanations of their sons' leadership abilities, but described daughters as being "bossy."[27]

Many Christian women know they have leadership gifts, but have difficulty admitting or accepting it. "I've always known I've had leadership gifts," one woman confessed, "but the title 'leader' intimidated me because, as a woman, I felt like I had to apologize for it. There've been a lot of times in my life when I was very aware that I had influence and impact, but various circumstances and people in my life made me want to hide it." When women shrink to fit others' expectations by hiding or denying their gifts, they fail to reach their full potential.

SHAME

I know something about shame. Shame was my close companion in the early days of my new life as a believer. Shame almost convinced me that it was too late to turn things around. Shame told me that I had gone too far for God to do anything truly significant through me. Shame told me that the only people God used were ones who did not make the mistakes I had. Shame told me I was useless and unwanted, a reject or misfit. Those are the things that shame says.

Christie Love has an acronym for shame: Satan Hammering At Me Endlessly. As the founder and executive director of LeadHer, a ministry devoted to helping women reach their God-given potential, Christie believes shame is one of the biggest struggles facing women today. Not only has she seen it at work in the lives of women she ministers to, she has dealt with it personally.

Shame is not just what we bring upon ourselves; sometimes other people heap shame upon us. In the period following her divorce, Christie wondered if God could still use her. Over time, she worked through the issues of personal shame and guilt, believing that God uses broken and flawed people, but others doubted. "After many years, I still felt disqualified at church. It's one of the saddest things to me because as the body [of Christ] we have to be better at reflecting grace. There are lots of women in that situation, and the body of Christ is not always a safe place to fall."

Donna, the vice president of Living Bridge Media at Insight for Living, had a similar experience: "I will never forget one [person] at church who told me she thought it was wonderful that Insight for Living hired divorced people. Sheesh! You are [already] having to go through all the self-examination that has to take place to heal from a divorce, so there is a lot of doubt whether you will ever fit in without [others making you feel] like a fifth wheel or [heaping on] the stigma that comes from a divorce."

There are times when guilt is appropriate, when sorrow leads to repentance. "For godly grief produces a repentance that leads to salvation without regret" (2 Cor. 7:10). But shame-based thinking prevents us from attaining our full potential because our defects and faults are ever before us.

CONCLUSION

Like Debbie Jonnes and so many women, you may doubt your abilities as a leader. You may doubt that you're a leader at all. Maybe you suspect you have leadership abilities, but no one has ever taken the time to nurture them into life. If that is you — if you have ever felt invisible, unappreciated, please know you are not invisible to God. Or maybe, like Sarah and Shawna, you have hidden your leadership gifts. Maybe you do not know what to do with all that strength. Or maybe, like Christie, you are mired in shame. Maybe you cannot imagine the good God could do with a life like yours.

"You are the light of the world," Jesus tells us. "A city set on a hill cannot be hidden. Nor do people light a lamp and put it under a basket, but on a stand, and it gives light to all in the house. In the same way, let your light shine before others, so that they may see your good works and give glory to your Father who is in heaven" (Matt. 5:14–16). Whatever the truth may be, do not let it keep you from letting your light shine.

In this chapter, we have looked at what leadership means today, from both a secular and a biblical perspective. We have also talked about three reasons why women fail to see themselves as leaders. Despite these obstacles, more Christian women are leading now than ever before. In the next chapter, we will take a look at where female Christian leaders are flourishing.

CHAPTER 3
THE INVISIBLE ARMY

HOW GOD IS USING CHRISTIAN WOMEN

Vision is the art of seeing the invisible.

—Jonathan Swift

The most ancient tool of warfare is not the sword or the scythe—it's smoke. For millennia, warring groups have exploited smoke to obscure movement in areas that were open to enemy fire. Nobody knows exactly when smoke became a strategic military tactic, but the Greek historian Thucydides records that it concealed some of the battles in the Peloponnesian War in the fifth century.

The term *smoke screen* has long been an American colloquialism. We use it to describe that which clouds or hides the truth. The theological debate over the role of women inadvertently serves as a smoke screen that eclipses the way God is using influential Christian women around the world. Christian women are God's invisible army. As we discussed in the last chapter, the theological debate about female leaders is important, but it needs to take place in the context of a larger, celebratory conversation about how God is working through women. Otherwise, the stories of these women are lost, and our lack of stories truncates our vision of what God can do through a single life — your life, my life, and the lives of our daughters.

BEHIND THE SMOKE SCREEN

In his book *Junia Is Not Alone*, Scot McKnight argues that the church has been silent regarding how God worked through women in the Scriptures. Two decades of teaching college students who, for the most part, grew up in church convinced him that "churches don't talk about the women of the Bible. Of Mary mother of Jesus they have heard, and even then not all of what they have heard is accurate. But of the other woman saints of the Bible ... they have heard almost nothing."[1]

McKnight is right that churches have largely silenced the voices of women throughout church history, but he is also correct in pointing out that the same thing is happening today because the stories and contributions of women continue to be marginalized, not only within the church but also, as we saw in the first chapter, in the cloistered halls of academia.

But there is a way to peek behind the smoke screen. By piecing together the little we do know about influential Christian women from a handful of studies and stories, we can get a small glimpse of how God is using Christian women in Christian education, churches, and parachurch organizations. This chapter is a dance of sorts between numbers and story.[2]

But the numbers are important because they show us what is happening to Christian women on a global scale. When you look at the numbers on women in both secular and Christian spheres, it is easy to get discouraged. Some think that the numbers are so disheartening to women that they are giving up, because fewer women are pursuing graduate degrees across most disciplines. Experts think that the steady stream of studies and statistics about the glacial (or altogether static) progress of female leaders in the twenty-first century is a deterrent from seeking further education or pursuing higher levels of leadership. Women are either giving up on their dreams or learning to dream different (and, some argue, less ambitious) dreams.

That is why stories are so important. If numbers are the telescope that gives us the vast, macroscopic picture, the stories of Christian female leaders are the microscope that gives us the minute, detailed picture. We are hardwired for stories. We tell them around the breakfast table and the watercooler, over the phone and the internet, and at bedtime as we tuck our children in for the night. Stories are the way we experience the world, the way we make sense of the world, and they humanize abstract principles and statistics. Anthropologists estimate that 70 percent of what we learn is through stories.[3]

In ancient Israel, the telling of stories was so important that several feasts were held throughout the calendar year to commemorate — to remember the story of — God's faithfulness to the Israelites. After the nation of Israel passed over the Jordan River, the Lord instructed Joshua to set up memorial stones in the dry riverbed, "that this may be a sign among you. When your children ask in time to come, 'What do those stones mean to you?' then you shall tell them that the waters of the Jordan were cut off before the ark of the covenant" (Josh. 4:6–7). As Matthew Henry comments, "The works of the Lord are so worthy of remembrance, and the heart of man is so prone to forget them, that various methods are needful to refresh our memories."[4]

Stories are the cement that paves our expectations and firms up our faith, shaping our understanding of what is real and what is possible.

CHRISTIAN EDUCATION

Dr. Mimi Barnard knows the importance of formal theological training, and she knows how hard it is for women to advance to upper levels of leadership in these schools. In her former role as vice president for professional development for the Council of Christian Colleges and Universities, she attended the American Council on Education's National Leadership Forum, where she learned that though "women earn the majority of all college degrees and are well represented in entry- and mid-level positions ... they have made little progress advancing to boardrooms and executive suites."[5]

Despite the contemporary trend to eschew seminary altogether,[6] the leaders of tomorrow are, for the most part, hewn rocks drawn from the quarries of our educational institutions. Ideally, our seminaries and Christian universities form the people who shape and lead our culture, training them to think clearly and critically while molding their understanding of the universe and our place in it.

Given the significance of formal theological training, let's look first at the number of female students attending these schools as well as the number of female faculty employed in these schools to have a better overall understanding of women's leadership roles in Christian organizations.

The Association of Theological Schools (ATS) is an organization of more than 250 seminaries and other graduate schools of theology from various faith traditions located in the United States and Canada. Since 1972, women's enrollment in master's and doctoral programs has steadily increased from 12.5 percent in 1972 to 34 percent in 2011. Thirty percent of these female students are enrolled in a master of divinity program, while the remaining 70 percent are pursuing other ministerial leadership or doctoral degrees.[7] This is an average of all ATS schools; there are member schools almost entirely made up of female students and others where women are a very small minority.

The number of female students in ATS schools is lower than the number of women enrolled in law (47%) or medicine (48%), where women make up almost half of the student body. Yet in both law and medical schools, the number of female students has declined since a peak in the 2001–2002 school year, while the enrollment for women in ATS-affiliated schools has continued slowly to rise.

The Council for Christian Colleges and Universities (CCCU) is an international higher education association comprised of 116 "intentionally Christian" universities and colleges in the US. In these schools, women make up 60 percent of the total student body, but these numbers are spread across multiple undergraduate and graduate degree programs, many of which are not related to biblical, theological, or ministerial leadership fields.

But what is most troubling is that the gender gap is even greater among the faculty and senior administrators at both ATS- and CCCU-affiliated schools. Though the number of full-time female faculty in ATS schools has grown from a paltry 3.2 percent in 1972 to a modest 24 percent in 2012, very little progress has been made since 2002, when the percentage of female faculty was 22.3 percent. Likewise, on CCCU campuses, women make up only 17 percent of senior administrators and 41 percent of full-time faculty.

The issues of women in Christian higher education are deeply complex. On the one hand, the numbers seem to indicate that progress has been made. On the other hand, progress has stalled and obstacles for women remain real. Mimi Barnard, now an assistant provost at Belmont College in Nashville, Tennessee, states, "There is not a fair process for women. There's rhetoric about a fair process, but the standards are too high for women, and too low for men. Women take on all the work—too much work—and don't get paid as much as men who don't work as hard but get rewarded more."

Belmont's university tagline is "From here to anywhere." As the assistant provost of interdisciplinary studies and global education, Mimi supervises three majors and a graduate program as well as builds global partnerships for study abroad programs. Her high energy and aptitude for working with internal and external stakeholders help her to pull together the various pieces involved in her work. From the beginning, Mimi has been a collaborative leader, seeking faculty input and empowering them to be creative in their roles as educators.

Mimi is an effusive communicator who manages, thanks to her Texas roots, to be both no-nonsense and intensely warm and relatable. Among other women, Mimi has always felt a bit like an outlier. Even as a young wife and mom, she wanted to talk about public policy and work opportunities and was frustrated with the typical conversations at women's Bible studies. "I'm older now, and I have less patience for those conversations.... I'm fifty-two and embracing a future that's exciting and challenging. I don't try to change my peers as I would have ten years ago because it's not my job to change every situation. I just want to use my gifts!"

Dr. Sue Edwards, an associate professor of education at Dallas Theological Seminary (DTS), is one of the 24 percent of female faculty employed at an ATS school. She started out by volunteering to put together a women's ministry for a large church in Plano, Texas. "I worked sixty hours a week but never went to a staff meeting. I was never part of the team and I really grieved over that." Eventually, she was hired by Irving Bible Church, where she served as the pastor to women for seven years before DTS pulled her into a professorate.

At first, Sue's biggest challenge at DTS was the lack of receptivity among some of the male faculty. "Initially, there were some men uncomfortable with a woman as a professor, but not many. I've been there full-time for eight years, and I'm tenured now. Some men struggled to see the value of what a woman can bring, but the men in my department have all been very supportive."

The greatest blessing she has received from her job has been watching men begin to view women differently. Some students are surprised to have a female professor, but by the end of the semester, Sue has won them over. "They stopped looking at me as a woman but as someone who can help them be fully equipped for ministry."

Across the world in Adoor, India, one of *National Geographic*'s "top ten paradises of the world," Dr. Annie George works as a biblical studies and ministry professor at Faith Theological Seminary. Her father founded the school with twenty-four students back in 1970 to provide a six-month training program for young men who wanted to plant churches. He quickly realized that more than six months were needed, so he expanded the curriculum. Today, the student body has grown to 180 (130 male, 50 female) and the curriculum includes a bachelor's degree in divinity, several master's degrees, and, soon, a doctoral theology program.

Annie radiates a type of calm, assured serenity. Being in ministry was never part of Annie's plan. From an early age, she wanted to be an engineer, but she received a call to ministry in the second year of her degree. When Annie is not teaching at the seminary, she is preaching. She oversees the children's and women's ministries at Lifetime Vineyard Church and is often called upon to teach classes and preach on Sunday mornings. "I can get more opportunities if I want. I train Sunday school teachers and, because I'm a professor, people call me to preach outside my church. But these are new trends … even in a Pentecostal church. Women are not usually allowed to preach, especially from the pulpit on Sunday."

Annie believes God has called her to teach in seminary and in the local church to help the churches in India grapple with the external and internal struggles they are facing. "There's a lot of opposition to ministry in India right now … sometimes passive, sometimes aggressive." Like churches in the West, churches in India wrestle with superficial spirituality, materialism, and individualism. "Now our society is moving to where there is more divorce. There's a lot of family problems and a lot of brokenness." These needs fuel Annie's passion for ministry. "I enjoy teaching," Annie says. "I enjoy caring for other people, being with them when they are sick, and counseling them."

PROTESTANT CHURCHES

Dr. Jackie Roese was born and raised in upstate New York, but she has a personality the size of Texas. She made waves in the

Dallas—Fort Worth metroplex when, after an eighteen-month study, the elders—all men—of Irving Bible Church made her the first female preacher to fill the pulpit in the church's forty-year history. The decision rattled a lot of cages—so much so that the church had a bodyguard stand by, but Jackie was glad the elders were willing to give the decision its due diligence. "Too often elders take an hour or day to make this decision. Our elders took almost two years," she said. "It deserved that kind of time and energy before [they were finally comfortable] in saying it seemed Scripture allowed women to preach under the authority of the elders."

We know that there are roughly 100 billion galaxies in the universe, 50 billion planets in our galaxy, seven billion people living on earth, 100 trillion cells in the human body, and about 320,000 churches in the United States. Yet despite our staggering amount of knowledge, we cannot say for sure just how many women are serving in leadership positions in Protestant churches—let alone conservative evangelical churches—in the United States.

Figuring out the actual number of Christian women leading in Protestant, evangelical churches is complicated, if not impossible, for four reasons. First, Christian women are not typically the focus of research studies. Second, the Protestant faith has fractured into so many different denominations that there is not a single association from which one can easily draw a reliable sample of all denominations and churches. Third, many denominations (especially smaller denominations) do not assess or report leadership demographics. Fourth, many women are leading in churches in ways that are technically "off the books," in volunteer or associate levels of leadership.

That said, there are a couple of studies that show us approximately how many women are serving as senior pastors in churches across the country. In 2009, through their denominationally balanced annual tracking survey, the Barna Group found that the percentage of female senior pastors serving in Protestant churches had doubled from 5 percent in 1999 to 10 percent in 2009. Most women (58 percent) serving in the pastorate are affiliated with mainline churches.[8] In 2010, the Hartford Institute for Religion Research found that of all congregations, 12 percent of senior pastors were women,[9] but in evangelical churches, that number fell to 9 percent.[10]

Again, these numbers are estimates of *female senior pastors*, which is a very small portion of all female leaders serving within the church. The actual number of female leaders serving at all levels within the church is probably much higher, especially because these numbers do not include women like Jackie who hold leadership positions within the church, and even preach from the pulpit on Sunday mornings, but are not senior pastors. The truth is we do not have the numbers of Christian women serving as leaders in churches.

Jackie's journey to the teaching pastorate at Irving Bible Church began with a Bible study she led at home. For two years, six women gathered to learn what the Scriptures said about everything from grace to Satan. "The women shared their doubts about whether God was real or that Jesus was the only way," Jackie remembers. "I spent hours digging through boxes in my garage, looking for this resource book or that one. I knew I was in over my head so I prayed—a lot."

Eventually, the group connected to the Women's Ministry at Irving Bible Church, and there the leader, Sue Edwards, noticed that Jackie had a gift for teaching. "Sue was always looking to develop women," Jackie said. "So it wasn't surprising when she eventually asked me to teach a message at the women's Bible study. I remember that when she asked, I said no in my head, but yes came out of my mouth. Kind of shocked me." When Sue left Irving Bible to teach at Dallas Seminary, Jackie took on the role of teaching pastor to women. She served in that role for more than fifteen years before launching the Marcella Project, an online organization committed to helping women become critical spiritual thinkers.

Meko Kapchinsky is the college and young adult pastor at Granite

Creek Community Church in Claremont, California. Meko's affinity for deep theological reflection and conversation is what draws her to college-aged people, because it is the time in life when many begin asking difficult questions. "I'm passionate about partnering with the eighteen- to thirty-year-old crowd," she says, "and helping them develop a faith that is their own as opposed to their parents'."

She did not start out with the title of *pastor*; it was something she "vigorously lobbied" for. She was motivated not out of a desire for prestige but rather out of a longing for legitimacy. "My father-in-law (the senior pastor) asked, 'Why do you need the title? You're already doing the work.' But I wanted to elevate [the college and young adult] ministry to that level—that it was a legit ministry with a legit purpose."

Meko's passion for the college crowd began when she was working at Azusa Pacific University (APU) in university marketing. "We had a plethora of interns coming through our office at university marketing," Meko said. "I just resonated with these kids and empathized with where they were in life. They were trying to discover who they were, figure out what they wanted to be when they grew up, figure out if their faith was their own."

When she quit APU to stay at home with her daughter, she missed that daily connection. During this same period, her church had been cycling through several college/young adult pastors, and Meko decided that God was calling her to step into that role. "When I finally started the group, I just felt like this is what I was supposed to be doing. Of course, that's not to say that every day is poops and giggles. The Millennials are a fickle, fickle bunch, and I think this is one of the hardest ministry demographics to minister to."

PARACHURCH ORGANIZATIONS

Phyllis Hendry knew early on she wanted to be a pastor like her father, Joe, a Baptist preacher in Fort Meade, Florida. She would line up her teddy bears in neat little rows and preach a sermon on the law of God, and she would go with her father on Saturday morning visitations. From preaching to providing spiritual care and direction to building relationships, she loved everything about the role of a pastor and was sure that that was what she was going to do with her life.

Her parents and mentors told her she could do anything she wanted to do with her life, until she told them she wanted to preach. "We didn't mean that," she recalls them saying. "The church was the first place I encountered what might be called a glass ceiling." So Phyllis took her leadership talents to the business world and started in banking, where she was asked to lead whole departments way back in the time when women were not allowed to wear pants to work. "People saw I was willing to work hard and work with people on my team. I think that's the only thing I can think of that's brought me to these levels in leadership."

Today, Phyllis is president and CEO of Lead Like Jesus, a nonprofit ministry "developing leaders who lead as Jesus led, so that the world will come to know Jesus." Like Phyllis, many gifted women who felt their leadership gifts were not being fully utilized at church have found a place of influence in one of the thousands of Christian nonprofits around the world.

The Christian Leadership Alliance (CLA) is a biblically centered association with more than five thousand individuals serving in more than four thousand Christian nonprofit organizations, including Focus on the Family, the Navigators, World Vision, Best Christian Workplaces, *Christianity Today*, Compassion International, SIM USA, the Salvation Army, Samaritan's Purse, and MOPS.

In analyzing the CLA membership directory, I found that men outnumbered women by more than two to one, with males comprising 68 percent of all members. Of the female members, 59 percent hold some type of leadership position in their organization, from the C-suite (such as CEO or CFO) down to first-line managers (such as office or department managers). Figure 1 shows a breakdown of the levels of leadership attained by women serving in these Christian organizations.

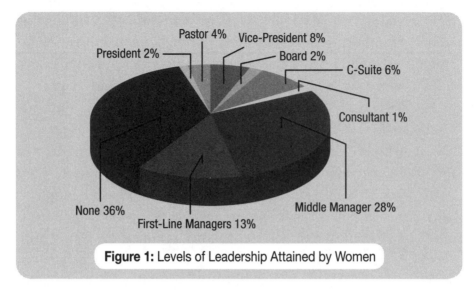

Figure 1: Levels of Leadership Attained by Women

Women make up only a third of all CLA members, but of that third, 63 percent have some sort of leadership role in their organization if you include pastors. But even that number is Panglossian in the sense that the type of woman who would be a member of the Christian Leadership Alliance is most likely a leader. Meaning, the percentage of women serving as leaders across all CLA organizations is probably much less than 63 percent.

For the sake of comparison, figure 2 gives the breakdown for male members.

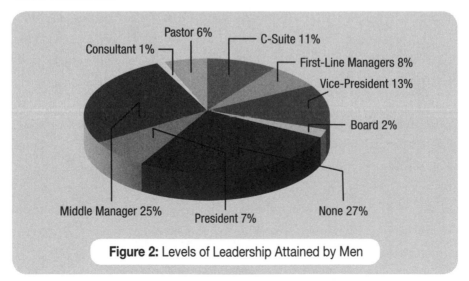

Figure 2: Levels of Leadership Attained by Men

As you can see, including the same groups as before, the percentage of male members holding leadership positions is 73 percent, a full 10 percent more than female members. Even more interesting (or not, depending on how you look at it), 33 percent of male leaders hold positions in upper management (C-suite, president, VP, and board member) compared with 18 percent of women. When it comes to middle managers or first-line managers, women outnumber men 41 percent to 33 percent. Since women are more commonly found in first-line manager positions than upper-level leadership positions, this means that fewer women actually break through "the stained-glass ceiling" in Christian parachurch organizations.

But here is where the story tells a little more than the numbers. "I will say," Phyllis commented, "I've never encountered a glass ceiling in the business world . . . if I did, I think I ignored it. I'd say, 'This is what needs to be done, and I'm going to do it.' I did what I believed was the right thing at the right time for where I was and the organization was." Leadership has usually been a progression for Phyllis. "At Lead Like Jesus, I came in as a president, but normally it's a progression that comes through relationship and team building. I started out as the business manager at National Science Center, then became the director, and then the president. It was a progression."

But what's most surprising about Phyllis, to me, is her personality. She does not seem like a C-suite type of gal. She's thoughtful, engaging, and pensive: every bit as fitting in a pastoral role as a presidency. Her aquamarine eyes shimmer with genuine interest and concern for others. It is clear that Phyllis Hendry *sees* people. "My father had an influence on me: he taught me how to build relationships and see potential in people. He taught me that if we help each other, we can grow to be the best."

Julie Slagter is founder of the Michigan Abolitionist Project (MAP), a grassroots organization dedicated to preventing local human trafficking through education and awareness. Julie began to sense God's call to be an advocate for women and children while working with college students at Cran-Hill Ranch, a Christian camp located an hour north of Grand Rapids. While she attended Grand Rapids Theological Seminary, a professor connected her with a ministry in Athens, Greece, that worked with men and women in prostitution who were often trafficked from Nigeria or Eastern European countries.

What began as a three-month commitment became a full year, and when Julie returned to the US, she sought discernment on what to do next. "I was concerned about people who were going in and out of brothels and deeply connected to the issues of modern-day slavery and human trafficking. The international ministry The Evangelical Alliance Mission (TEAM) was active in more than fifty countries, but most of those ministries are refugee ministries—the only anti-slavery one is in Greece." Julie knew more proactive anti-slavery ministries were needed, so she became a global coordinator of End Slavery with International Teams, traveling internationally to train workers to get the fledgling ministry off the ground.

During that time, Julie became concerned about the human trafficking situation in her hometown. "I needed to know what prostitution looks like in West Michigan. I got frustrated with the whole 'It's just happening over there' mentality. I wondered, what does it really look like in West Michigan?" Julie started acting locally, founding MAP with a handful of others in a local Panera. "We're committed to staying focused on prevention—there is already aftercare. We want to educate people: What are red flags? What is a yellow flag? How should I interpret different situations I may come across?"

Emily Chengo, a native Kenyan, is the African director for African Leadership and Reconciliation Ministries (ALARM), an organization that trains leaders across east and central Africa in biblical theology, conflict resolution, forgiveness, mediation, leadership skills, and reconciliation. Emily has always been driven by a desire to transform communities through microenterprises. "I want to work with communities and bring change through microenterprises. My MBL thesis on microfinance was a bridge for me to community transformation."

Growing up, Emily was taught that leadership was for men, and the role of women was to submit. "When I started taking leadership positions, I thought it was not the right thing to be a leader ... I would resist leadership positions that came to me." But God's calling refused to be shut out of her life. "I realized it's not about the gender but about the calling. I'm a mother, a wife, and there is much more a woman can do in society. At ALARM, we model that and help others to walk in that calling."

Soon after receiving a master's degree in business leadership from the University of South Africa, Emily began supervising microenterprise initiatives for international nongovernment organizations (NGOs). She eventually joined ALARM because they had a program to work with women. "As God would have it, I rose up to become the African director ... but what really brought me here is to work with women to transform their life."

Emily oversees the work of ALARM in eight countries—Kenya, Uganda, Sudan, South Sudan, Rwanda, Burundi, Congo, and Tanzania. ALARM's strategic programs are at once comprehensive and extensive. Emily's team travels throughout each country identifying communities in need of transformation and individuals who are likely to help bring that change. "We like to develop leaders beginning with the church," Emily says, "because churches are in every community. They go back and transform their communities, sharing what they learn in our program with others." ALARM also initiates reconciliation between various groups by establishing schools between warring communities and identifying sources of conflict—like water resources. "It's the by-product of developing leaders and dealing with issues of reconciliation.... We'll actually sink wells in communities that had a problem with water."

But Emily is most drawn to the work ALARM does for women, instructing them in leadership development and microenterprise. "In Nairobi, I've seen women go from the slums to grow to such a level that they open a bank account. In Uganda, some women used to work in the quarry breaking stones, but now they make beads. They meet around Bible studies to learn it's not just about money but about growing [spiritually]."

As a leader, Emily thinks her greatest strength is to encourage others. "I encourage people a lot," she says, "because I know there is potential. Women are told, you cannot manage, you cannot be leaders—including myself. I came a long way. You have to develop yourself first to become a leader."

CONCLUSION

God is working through women. I want my daughters to know that. I want them to know that *their lives count before God.* I want them to know that they are full of tremendous potential to be a force for good to a world swamped in incomprehensible evil. Most of all, I want them to know that they are not invisible to God. I want you to know that too. *You matter.* Even in those moments when you feel most useless, most irrelevant, most unwanted, most unqualified or disqualified, *you are not invisible to God.* God, the Creator of a universe that contains a staggering 100 billion galaxies—sees you, and he has gifted you for a specific purpose. "But each has his own gift from God," the apostle Paul writes, "one of one kind and one of another.... Only let each person lead the life that the Lord has assigned to him, and to which God has called him" (1 Cor. 7:7, 17).

To grow as leaders, we need to have a firm grasp of the challenges we will encounter. Women today live in a time of unparalleled freedom and opportunity. Though women are still underrepresented in top leadership positions in every sector of American life, from politics to business to the church, the truth is that we have more opportunities to have a meaningful impact on our world and our society today than at any other time in human history. But many challenges remain, especially for Christian women.

Over the years, I have met many female Christian leaders looking for help on how to lead and how to navigate the terrain they find themselves in. Some women, especially young women, have trouble discerning what God is calling them to do with their lives. Some feel unprepared for the positions they find themselves in; others feel excluded from informal networks; many struggle to balance home and work/ministry; some wonder how to build strong relationships with men and women; others struggle with perceptions about their leadership and their identity as women.

These challenges are real and they are great and they have to be addressed if we hope to move forward as faithful stewards of our spiritual gifts. In the next chapter, we examine the first challenge for female Christian leaders: navigating the mysterious process of discerning God's calling on our lives.

CHAPTER 4
CALLING

WHAT IS MY LIFE FOR?

This little light of mine, I'm gonna let it shine!
I'm not gonna make it shine, I'm just gonna let it shine.
Out in the dark, I'm gonna let it shine.

The last gasp of summer seeped in through the cracked weather stripping of our old Ford pickup truck as my dad and I drove north on Highway 69 from Mineola to Quitman, Texas. It was the time of year when summer starts fading into fall. Dad was listening to some country crooner on the radio as I watched the evergreen forests blur past my window, thinking about how my life was going to change. The next week, I was starting preschool. And just like that, there would be no more daily trips to the sandy creek, no more trips to the lake, no more adventures on the playground of Nanny's Playhouse.

"Daddy," I finally asked, "why do I have to go to preschool?"

"Preschool? So you can go to elementary school."

"And elementary school?"

"So you can go to high school."

"And high school?"

"So you can go to college."

"And college?"

"So you can get a job."

"Daddy, why do I have to get a job?"

"So you can live."

"But, Daddy, when do I get to *really live*?"

Though I did not have the ability then to verbalize it, what I really wanted to know was, "What's my life for?" Surely it must be for something more than school and a job.

Of all the creatures on earth, humans are the only species with the ability to reflect on the purpose of their existence. No one, not even the agnostic or the atheist, can escape from the fundamental questions: What does my life mean? What is it for? Philosophers, artists, and common, everyday people have wrestled with discerning the meaning of life from time immemorial. And the answers abound—from Plato's human flourishing through the cultivation of virtues, to Epicurus's pleasure-seeking and freedom from fear, to the postmodern idea that the meaning of life is relative to the individual because it means whatever you want it to mean.

Even amid a myriad of answers, it is true that some of us do not want to know what our lives are for, but the question still presses in on us. We distract ourselves with television, video games, the internet, shopping, crowded schedules, a carousing lifestyle, or various addictions. Without meaning, our lives are adrift in an endless sea, rudderless, powerless against the great tides of history and culture.

For Christians, finding the meaning, the calling, of our lives anchors us to the world by showing us our rightful place within it.

Calling answers the question of life's meaning because it tells us what we should do with our lives, how we should spend these brief years, days, and hours that the Lord has given us.

For female Christian leaders, then, the first obstacle is discerning, with crystal clarity, the calling God has placed upon our lives. In this chapter, we will discuss the nature and purpose of calling, specific strategies for discerning our calling, and the importance of stewarding our calling well.

WHAT IS CALLING?

When I was young, I spent a lot of time on baseball fields, swinging bats and chasing fly balls. I was never any good. But there were a couple of beautiful moments when I swung that baseball bat and the ball connected with the bat's sweet spot, sending that ball flying out of the park.

The sweet spot is the place on a baseball bat that results in maximum performance for the effort you put into it. Whenever you hit a baseball, vibrations travel in waves up and down the length of the bat, and much of the energy is lost. But hitting the ball with the sweet spot of the bat produces a lot less vibration, so more of the energy sends the ball soaring into the outfield.

Living out our calling is like hitting a ball with the sweet spot of a baseball bat: we get maximum results for the energy we expend because our gifts are perfectly matched to a particular ministry need. The experience is comparable to what psychology professor Mihaly Csikszentmihalyi describes as *flow*, "the state in which people are so involved in an activity that nothing else seems to matter; the experience itself is so enjoyable that people will do it even at great cost, for the sheer sake of doing it."[1] When you are in a state of flow, there is a sense that you were born to do this. That is what calling feels like. But exactly what is it?

There are two aspects of calling. We first receive the "upward" call of repentance and salvation from the Lord, inviting us into a reconciled relationship with him. We then receive a second call, in which we are called to a particular role in the building of his kingdom. We are first called into the family of God; then we are called out into the world to bring others into a relationship with God. When we talk about a calling to ministry leadership, we are talking about the second calling.

Prior to the Reformation, having a calling meant one was called to the priesthood and a life of celibacy. With the Reformation came the emphasis on the priesthood of all believers. Though not all believers are church workers or pastors, all believers are priests who "can come into the presence of God through the blood of the Lamb ... can handle holy things (such as the Bible, earlier denied to the laity) ... and can proclaim the gospel."[2]

According to Martin Luther, there is no difference between the priest and the laity except for the official role of "priest." "It is pure invention that pope, bishops, priests, and monks are to be called the 'spiritual estate'; princes, lords, artisans and farmers the 'temporal estate.' That is indeed a fine bit of lying and hypocrisy.... All Christians are truly of the 'spiritual estate,' and there is among them no difference at all but that of office."[3]

" 'The priesthood of all believers,' " writes author Gene Edward Veith, "did not make everyone into church workers; rather, it turned every kind of work into a sacred calling."[4] This new understanding of vocation infused sacred meaning into everyday life. No longer were marriage and family considered low and abased, but places rich with opportunity for spiritual growth and service. No longer were farmers and blacksmiths, artists and bakers viewed as secular workers, but people with the opportunity to serve God by serving others through their vocations.

In his book *The Teaching Ministry of Congregations*, Princeton professor Richard Robert Osmer defines *calling* or *vocation* as the "individual's calling to partnership with God in which particular gifts are evoked and developed in concert with their discernment of the particular role God has given them to play during a certain period of their lives."[5] Calling is not just related to ministry, though that is often the first thing we think of, but it refers also to our roles as spouses, parents, workers, and citizens.

God is calling all believers, including Christian women, to flourish in their giftedness. There is no real ministry—whether it is pastoring, mentoring, teaching, or evangelizing—that does not emerge out of the spiritual gifts God bestows on all believers, men and women alike.

Faithfully stewarding our spiritual gifts often means leading, regardless of whether one serves in a complementarian or egalitarian context. Whether you are mentoring, raising or leading children, teaching, serving in a pastoral role, heading up women's ministry, or leading as an executive in a nonprofit Christian ministry, you are functioning as a leader out of the abundance of your spiritual giftedness.

WHY ARE WE CALLED?

In his children's book, *The Selfish Giant*, Oscar Wilde tells the story of a selfish giant who wanted to keep his garden all to himself. Every afternoon, the children stopped by to play in the giant's garden because it was lovely and large, with soft green grass and peach trees that bore delicious fruit. The children were always happy there—until one day, the giant expelled the children from the garden.[6]

Nobody was allowed in the garden but the giant himself. Without the garden, the children had nowhere to play. Winter came to the giant's garden and never left. The birds did not come, the trees did not bear fruit, and the flowers did not bloom because the children were not there. When the giant realized how selfish he had been, he welcomed the children back to the garden and spring returned, melting the snow, ice, and frost.

It is a story we have heard many times, from Dickens's *A Christmas Carol* to *Pay It Forward* to *Bruce Almighty*, the story of individuals who are afraid or unwilling to give, clinging to wealth and gifts with clenched fists until, after a painful period of growth, they are able to offer up their gifts with an open palm. In a competitive, self-centered, inward-focused world, it is a story that cannot be told too many times.

In an analysis of 766,513 books published between 1960 and 2008, researchers discovered a growing emphasis on "me" rather than "we." When comparing individualistic phrases like "me against the world" or "I am special" to communal phrases like "it takes a village" or "community spirit," researchers found an emphasis on a certain type of individualism. "There's an emphasis on uniqueness and greatness, and things being personalized for the individual," psychologist Jean Twenge comments. "But it's not about being independent and standing on your own two feet."[7]

Individualism is a bit like salt—a little is a good thing because it augments the flavors in, say, a huge pot of pinto beans; but too much and the beans are ruined, fit only for the compost pile. A little individualism encourages us to pursue our unique gifts and build a personal relationship with God; too much individualism and we think it is all about ourselves. Unfortunately, too much individualism has crept into some of the current teachings on calling.

In his book *Let Your Life Speak*, Parker Palmer leads us on an inner journey to discovering our calling or vocation. Palmer rightly encourages us to determine our calling by paying attention to our strengths and weaknesses, to discard our masks and find out who we are at the fundamental level. But Palmer's vision of vocation focuses like a laser beam upon the self, with very little regard for community or the context into which we are called.

He says, "Vocation does not come from a voice 'out there' calling me to become something I am not. It comes from a voice 'in here' calling me to be the person I was born to be, to fulfill the original selfhood given me at birth by God."[8] He says that we have not followed our true vocation because others—our parents, teachers, and society—have imposed another vocation upon us. He leads us on an inner pilgrimage, but does not lead us back out. He does not show us the *why* of our calling beyond our own satisfaction. He tells us only half the truth.[9]

In a society overly preoccupied with self, finding many resources on calling from an individualistic perspective is not surprising. Palmer is not alone. While it is true that each person's calling is uniquely unrepeatable, we are called into a community and into a specific context and for a specific purpose. The purpose of our calling goes far beyond personal satisfaction. Personal satisfaction is an unexpected benefit, not the purpose, of fulfilling our calling. After I go on a long run or climb a mountain (or, when in Michigan, a sand dune), I often experience "runner's high," a euphoric sense of well-being brought on by a flood of endorphins. But I do not run for the high. I run to be strong, for clarity of mind, and to meet personal goals. The runner's high? That is just the bonus.

So it is with personal satisfaction and calling. We are not to live out our calling just because we find it deeply satisfying (though it often is). Gene Edward Veith writes, "The doctrine of vocation undermines conformity, recognizes the unique value of every person, and celebrates human differences; but it sets these individuals into a community with other individuals, avoiding the privatizing, self-centered narcissism of secular individualism."[10] What sounds like a small distinction could not be more significant, because sometimes our calling leads us to places we do not want to go. Sometimes God calls us to Nineveh, and to Nineveh we go even though we say no. Sometimes God calls us out to lonely places, out to the desert or to the waiting place, to the threshing floor during harvest, to Mount Moriah, before the king of Persia, to the Coliseum, to a hill called Golgotha.

Sometimes our calling will make us cry out as Jesus did, "Please, if there's any other way, let it be! Not *this*." That is why the purpose of our calling can never be personal satisfaction, because if it is, when God calls us to Nineveh or to Golgotha, we will not have the courage, the character, to say with Christ, "Nevertheless, not my will, but yours, be done" (Luke 22:42).

The simple, unadulterated truth is this: We have been called to *be like Jesus* and to be a conduit through which that likeness spreads to others. Our calling is not, as some would have us believe, to become more like ourselves. "If anyone would come after me," Jesus said, "let him deny himself and take up his cross daily and follow me. For whoever would save his life will lose it, but whoever loses his life for my sake will save it" (Luke 9:23–24).

This same theme of self-denial is threaded throughout the New Testament. The apostle Paul writes in Colossians, "You have died, and your life is hidden with Christ in God" (3:3), and in Galatians, "It is no longer I who live, but Christ who lives in me" (2:20). In 2 Corinthians, the apostle proclaims, "He died for all, that those who live might no longer live for themselves but for him who for their sake died and was raised" (5:15).

But it is in the surprising text of Ephesians chapter 4 that Paul hammers home one of the most significant passages on self-denial. Ephesians 4 is one of three main passages that teach about the spiritual gifts,[11] but Paul says something very different in this passage. In 4:11–12 he writes, "He gave the apostles, the prophets, the evangelists, the shepherds and teachers, to equip the saints for the work of ministry." In every other passage regarding the spiritual gifts, the gift is an *ability* given to an individual believer. Here Paul says that the *individual* is the gift that Christ gives to the church.

It is easier to live a divided life if we think of ourselves as individuals with specific gifts. As long as we are faithful in the area of our giftedness—teaching, preaching, leading, shepherding, giving generously to the poor and disenfranchised—we can keep some small area of our lives to ourselves.

"Everything else I have, I'll sacrifice to God," we reason, "but this one thing, I'll keep for myself." This was the perilous mistake of Ananias and Sapphira, who kept for themselves a portion of the proceeds from the sale of a piece of property. When confronted, both Ananias and Sapphira lied, and for this they died (Acts 5:1–11). New Testament professor Craig Keener comments, "God took the corporate purity of his people, and the importance of sincerity in claims to total commitment far more seriously than most Christians do today."[12]

But Ephesians 4 tells us that the whole of our lives—not just a part of them—is consecrated unto God. Though Paul is speaking

specifically about apostles, prophets, evangelists, and shepherd-teach-
ers, which are foundational gifts that support the whole ministry of the
church, the principle is no less true for believers with other gifts. *People
are God's gift to the church! Women are God's gift to the church!*

So whether you are a pastor, a teacher, a leader in a Christian ministry, a layperson, or a parent, your calling is to be like Jesus and to be
a conduit through which that likeness spreads to others. This does not
mean you lose your individuality to become part of a faceless collective;
this means you sacrifice your allegiance to yourself. The paradox is that
you cannot find your "true self" by looking for it, but only by looking
for Christ. "You have formed us for yourself," writes St. Augustine,
"and our hearts are restless until they find their rest in you."[13]

WHAT SHOULD I DO WITH MY LIFE?

What, then, should we do with our lives? How does my calling to
be like Jesus relate to the unique talents and the giftedness God has
given me? Infinite are the ways that Christ can work through his
people, and the way he works through one person will not be the
same way he works through another.

Arloa Sutter is imitating Christ in East Garfield Park, an urban
community a few miles west of Chicago. Arloa grew up on a farm,
where people took care of each other, so when she moved to the
city, seeing the dumpster-divers and panhandlers perplexed her.
"There was something not right about that," she remembers. So
Arloa launched Breakthrough Ministries.

The ministry began with a few church members serving daily
lunch in a small storefront on Chicago's north side. Today, Breakthrough operates two homeless shelters that serve nearly 1,000
homeless adults each year, provide 24,000 nights of shelter, serve
more than 70,000 meals, and distribute 10,000 bags of groceries to
low-income families in the neighborhood.

Paula Hays is imitating Christ in Chaing Mai, Thailand. Thailand
is a source, transit, and destination country for human trafficking and

is one of the countries with the largest amount of commercial sexual exploitation of children. Although children of all social and economic backgrounds are at risk of sexual abuse and exploitation, the risk is greatest for those living in economically depressed areas.

After visiting Thailand on vacation, Paula and her husband, Gary, sensed the Lord calling them to Thailand to minister. They quit their jobs in Seattle and moved to Thailand without a firm ministry plan, but it did not take long for them to launch Think Small, a foundation that uses drama, games, and performing arts to present the gospel to young children in Thailand. Paula is passionate about reaching children for Christ and preventing them from being trafficked. "Our goal is to get kids into a better environment before they get trafficked," Paula said. "The stories will break your heart—all the abuse, beatings, and sexual perversions [these kids suffer]."

Malachy Marie Williams is imitating Christ in New York City and in New Jersey. Malachy's day job is as a television producer, a role that has earned her five regional Emmy nominations and the McDonald's Black Media Legends award. But producing is not all that Malachy does; she is also the associate minister of worship and the arts at the First Baptist Church of Cranford/Elizabeth in New Jersey and an adjunct professor in theology, church history, and Christian education in the Certificate Program in Christian Ministry at New York Theological Seminary. She is a regular volunteer at the historic Bowery Mission in downtown New York City, where she preaches chapel messages for the homeless.

Nikki Brown is imitating Christ in Greenville, South Carolina. Nikki is the program development manager at American Leprosy Missions, a 106-year-old organization devoted to helping people with leprosy. Now often known as Hansen's disease, leprosy is a contagious disease that affects the skin, mucous membranes, and nerves, causing discoloration and lumps on the skin and, in severe cases, disfigurement and deformities. Left untreated, bacteria will destroy nerve endings, removing the body's ability to feel pain; without pain, it is impossible to avoid repeated injuries, especially to the extremities.

Leprosy is not just a first-century problem. Every two minutes, someone is diagnosed, mostly in Africa, Asia, and South America. American Leprosy Missions brings healing and hope to some of the world's most ostracized people by providing them with treatment and microcredit loans to start their own businesses.

These are just a handful of the ways that God is working through women around the country and the world. In each case, women are leading out of a combination of their spiritual gifts and natural gifts. Understanding these two things is critical when trying to discern what God is calling you to do with your life — or even just a specific period in your life.

SPIRITUAL GIFTS

Spiritual gifts "are gifts of God enabling the Christian to perform his or her (sometimes specialized) service" for the edification of all believers.[14] In *Work in the Spirit: Toward a Theology of Work*, Yale theology professor Miroslav Volf, like Luther, argues that spiritual gifts, or charisms, "are not the possession of an elite group within the Christian fellowship," but rather "the Spirit, who is poured out upon all flesh, imparts also charisms to all flesh: they are gifts given to the Christian community irrespective of the existing distinctions or conditions within it."[15]

Volf is alluding to the fact that the spiritual gifts are gender-neutral because the Holy Spirit bestows these spiritual gifts to all of humankind, regardless of gender or social status. Joel 2:28–29, which Peter quotes in his sermon at Pentecost, reads,

"It shall come to pass afterward,
    that I will pour out my Spirit on all flesh;
your sons and your daughters shall prophesy,
    your old men shall dream dreams,
    and your young men shall see visions.
Even on the male and female servants
    in those days I will pour out my Spirit."

The writings of the apostles Paul and Peter are sprinkled with descriptions of various spiritual gifts bestowed upon God's people, including Romans 12:6–8; 1 Corinthians 12:8–10; 1 Corinthians 12:28–30; 1 Corinthians 13:1–3; Ephesians 4:11–16; and 1 Peter 4:10–11. These various gift lists are summarized in the table.

THE BIBLICAL LISTS OF SPIRITUAL GIFTS

ROM. 12:6–8	1 COR. 12:8–10	1 COR. 12:28–30	1 COR. 13:1–3	EPH. 4:11–16	1 PETER 4:10–11
Prophecy	Prophecy	Prophecy	Prophecy	Prophets	
Serving					Serving
Teaching	Knowledge	Teaching	Knowledge	Pastor-Teacher	
Exhortation	Wisdom				Speaking
Giving			Giving		
Leadership		Leadership			
Mercy					
	Healing	Healing			
	Faith		Faith		
	Miracles	Miracles			
	Tongues	Tongues	Tongues		
	Discernment				
		Interpreting Tongues			

These passages, along with Joel's prophecy and Peter's sermon on the day of Pentecost, indicate that the spiritual gifts are distributed by the Holy Spirit to "all flesh," all human beings, regardless of age, gender, or ethnicity for the purpose of serving the church.

What does this mean for women? It means that *women are as likely as men to be gifted with any of the spiritual gifts*—including preaching, teaching, and leadership. It also means that women have an equal responsibility to mindfully steward that gifting, ensuring they are not allowing it to fade in strength because of neglect (1 Tim. 4:14; 2 Tim. 1:6).

NATURAL GIFTS

While spiritual gifts are given only to believers, natural gifts are special talents and abilities a person has regardless of their belief in God. Exploring your natural gifts can provide more clues to help you discover your calling. What do you love to do? What comes naturally to you? Maybe like my husband, Paul, you're good at getting into other people's worlds. You can understand them and relate to them. People with that gift make good counselors, social workers, or even novelists.

Maybe like Meagan Wood Harris, the assistant director of recruitment and outreach for Claremont School of Theology, you have a sharp, analytical mind that is able to unpack and untangle difficult philosophical concepts. People with gifts like that make good academics or professors. Maybe like Donna Jones, vice president of Living Bridge Media at Insight for Living, you have a keen business mind and you can follow through on decisions quickly. People with such gifts can serve Christian organizations well.

Our natural gifts are not always what comes easiest for us, because often our natural gifts can be more difficult for us than for other people, simply because we are so passionate about them. As German novelist Thomas Mann wrote, "A writer is a person for whom writing is more difficult than it is for other people."

Exploring your spiritual and natural gifts and also paying attention to the confirmation of others in regard to your abilities and gifted-ness will guide you in the process of discerning your calling.

DISCERNING YOUR CALLING

Discerning our ministry calling is complicated because many of us do not know what we are really, truly meant to do. It is not that we are ambivalent or indifferent; it is just that life gets so crowded that it is easy to get caught up putting out fires. There are so many ministry needs that it is easy to do what needs to be done *in the minute* rather than think strategically about how our giftedness fits with ministry needs.

Other times, we just get lost. "I just got lost," croons Chris Martin of Coldplay, "every river that I tried to cross, / every door I ever tried was locked." On that path we were so sure was the way, we ran right up against God's immovable no. And just like that, we are lost, unsure of ourselves and our place in God's world. It is easy to lose sight of the core purpose of our calling. In the early days of our faith, it seemed so clear compared to the opaqueness that can settle later in our life of faith, after the years have deposited the filmy layers of loss and disappointments.

Sometimes, life just takes an unexpected turn, and you wind up on a road you do not know and did not anticipate. (How did I get here, to this place?) We lose our bright-eyed innocence and, with it, our daring. We lose our health, a home, a job, a marriage, a child. In the very worst of cases, what we lose is hope, that confidence that everything really does work together for good in the end.

Sometimes it is not the losing but the *getting* that obscures our calling. We get married, get mortgages, get the demanding sched-ule of young parenthood. We get the promotion and, with it, more responsibility. Life becomes more complicated.

Thankfully, there are several steps we can take to discern our calling.

First, take stock of your spiritual and natural gifts. Like when I hit a ball with the wrong spot on the bat, I can expend a lot of energy in the counseling ministry at church because it is not the best use of my gifts. I am a tell-it-like-it-is truth-teller who all too often wastes little time getting straight to the point. Truth may indeed set you free, but it takes time to heal, to get well, and to get whole. My husband has been counseling a group of men for more than a year and a half. He has the giftedness to meet with them each week, working through their issues — often the same ones — over and over.

I cannot do that. Not like he can. No matter how much I would like to, no amount of energy I put into it will be as good as what comes naturally to him. So rather than force it or feel guilty for what I cannot do, I have learned to put my energy toward what comes most naturally — like stringing together words that tell the story of how God loves us and how he has strategically gifted *each one of us* to be a force for good on a spinning planet rife with sorrow and senseless cruelty.

Take time to deliberate on where you were when everything seemed to flow together, where it seemed as if you were doing exactly what you were meant to do. Maybe you were teaching a Bible class at your church, and you saw signs of recognition and discovery in the eyes of your students. Maybe you were in a library or an isolated place writing a book or an article, and all the words came together to form a new truth you had learned and were excited to share. Maybe you were wrestling with complicated ideas and were trying to understand how they related, or mattered, to those in need around you. Maybe you were serving Thanksgiving dinner to the poor families in your community or helping to build a home for a family in need. Where were you? What were you doing?

Second, pay attention to what moves you. What are the issues that most often grip your mind, the ones that seem to always be percolating on the back burner? What are the things that keep you up at night? In his book *Beyond Words*, Frederick Buechner poignantly advises, "Whenever you find tears in your eyes, especially unexpected tears, it is well to pay the closest attention. They are not only telling you something about the secret of who you are, but more often than not God is speaking to you through them of the mystery of where you have come from and is summoning you to where … you should go next."[16]

Like the force of attraction between opposite ends of a magnet, so we are drawn to the needs our giftedness can match.

Third, listen to the counsel of wise advisors. Our mentors, parents, teachers, peers, and other family members can often be reliable guides to discern our calling. Wise advisors can help us in two ways. First, they can help us evaluate our strengths and areas of giftedness. When Marie, a youth director, first applied for a job at her local church, she applied for a position as an assistant. She had attended her church for a long time and had taken an active role volunteering in the youth department. When church leaders saw her application, they encouraged her to apply for the newly opened youth director position. While Marie did not identify herself as a leader, her leadership gifts were obvious to those who knew her well.

Second, wise advisors can help us ascertain and accept our weaknesses. When Patricia first took on the role of women's minister, she felt obligated to run the ministry on her own, including planning and preparing for all the annual events and the bimonthly outreach program, training lay workers to serve in the outreach program, counseling women, and teaching the weekly Bible study. Before long, the cracks started to show in her performance, but Patricia was unwilling to accept it, convinced all she needed to do was try harder. Eventually, Patricia's friends helped her to discern that unlike counseling and her administrative duties, the teaching times were draining her energy. Their input gave her the confidence to release the weekly Bible study into the hands of a more gifted teacher so she could focus on building the program and counseling women.

Many women have confided stories similar to those of Marie and Patricia; they do not recognize their own giftedness and they feel buried under ministry obligations. Sometimes we cannot discern our call because we are too close to it, and wise advisors provide a neutral, bird's-eye view. When looking for counsel, be sure to consider only those who know you best and who have your best interest at heart.

The final and most important way to discern your calling is to seek God's will. Search the Scriptures and saturate your mind with his word. Maintain regular times for prayer. Jennifer was an attorney with a high-profile firm in Manhattan. Her salary afforded her a nice apartment and the ability to fund major ministry projects through her local church. But when she began to set aside times for prayer and Scripture reading, she realized that God was calling her to quit her lucrative job and employ her legal training and abilities at a ministry that provides aid to children in third-world countries. Jennifer believes that it was her growing relationship with God and the practice of seeking his will through prayer and the Scriptures that gave her clarity regarding her calling.

CONCLUSION

Set during the invasion of Normandy, or "D-Day," in World War II, the film *Saving Private Ryan* follows a group of United States Army Rangers, led by Captain John Miller, as they go behind enemy lines to rescue paratrooper James Francis Ryan, whose three brothers had been killed in action.

To accomplish the mission, the group travels through dangerous territory and engages in several deadly conflicts. In the end, six of the eight-member squad are killed in action. As Captain Miller dies, he whispers to Private Ryan, "James, earn this. Earn it." The end of the film is set during the present time, and Private Ryan is an elderly veteran visiting Arlington Cemetery with his family. As he stands beside Captain Miller's grave, he remembers the sacrifices of the Army Rangers and the last words of Captain Miller. Turning to his wife with tears in his eyes, he says, "Tell me I've led a good life. Tell me I'm a good man."

I cannot watch (or even think of) that scene in *Saving Private Ryan* with a dry eye. It may seem odd to reference a war movie in a chapter on our calling as Christian women, but for me, that scene elucidates so succinctly what Christ did for me, and what I, in turn, can do for him. The Army Rangers in *Saving Private Ryan* laid down their lives as a sacrifice to save a mother from burying all four of her sons. Private Ryan, in turn, by living well, laid down his life as a tribute to their sacrifice. While we cannot earn what Christ did for us any more than Private Ryan could really earn the sacrifice of those six men, by being faithful to our unique callings, we too can offer up *all* our lives to God as a tribute to Christ's sacrifice.

CHAPTER 5
GREAT EXPECTATIONS

On Not Being Everything *to* Everyone

"You mustn't wish for another life. You mustn't want to be somebody else. What you must do is this: 'Rejoice evermore. Pray without ceasing. In everything give thanks.'

"I am not all the way capable of so much, but those are the right instructions."

—Wendell Berry, *Hannah Coulter*

I began with the best intentions. One weekend when my daughter, Ellie, was just a baby, I planned to work at least ten hours on dissertation, crank out a 1,500-word article plus two blog posts, prepare for some upcoming interviews, dissect a single chapter of John Paul's Theology of the Body with a friend, and finally read (and write a book review of) three other books in preparation for an upcoming speaking engagement—all while my husband was away working out of town. While this schedule may seem crazy and chaotic to some, for me, this breakneck speed felt normal just a little under a year before. Anything less and I felt unaccomplished and downright bored.

Enter Ellie, Little Miss Marathon, who, on her very best days, slept three to four hours straight and ate only the minimum required for her age. For the previous six months (i.e., her whole life), we had been trying to figure out ways to get her to sleep and eat, but it seemed that all she wanted to do was go, go, go. Her energy levels made even me feel like a century-old centipede. And all this came to a roaring head that particular weekend. For twenty-four hours, Ellie screamed and fought off both sleep and food. Finally, I decided just to step back, relax, and let her decide how much she was going to eat and when. By Sunday, she was a new baby—both her eating and sleeping had regulated themselves into a more normal pattern. On the one hand, I felt successful in my role as a mother because my baby was now comfortable and content; on the other hand, though, I felt like a failure. Rather than focusing on what I had "done right," I honed in on all that was left undone—namely, every single thing on my to-do list.

Every year since 1972 (the height of the feminist movement), the United States General Social Survey has polled fifteen hundred men and women regarding various aspects of their lives. The participants cut across all education levels, income levels, and marital statuses. In one question, participants are asked, "How happy are you, on a scale of 1 to 3, with 3 being very happy, and 1 being not too happy?"

Across the board, women's level of happiness has progressively declined. And this study is just one of a handful of studies that point to the same problem: in the face of unparalleled growth in educational opportunities, greater financial stability, and progress in the work sphere, women are unhappier than they were pre-1970. Markus Buckingham at the *Huffington Post* aptly summarizes: "Wherever researchers have been able to collect reliable data on happiness, the finding is always the same: greater educational, political, and employment opportunities have corresponded to decreases in life happiness for women, as compared to men."[1]

These findings have understandably stirred up a great deal of discussion and debate, with many voices trying to make sense of the data. While no single theory can probably fully explain the trend, some researchers believe that women have more freedom today to be honest about their level of unhappiness than they did thirty years ago, while others argue that women's unhappiness points to escalating pressures in a global society. Wharton professors (and husband-and-wife research team) Betsy Stevenson and Justin Wolfers speculate that the decline in happiness for women is largely due to women's rising expectations for themselves. In other words, it is no longer sufficient to be a devoted "stay-at-home mom" or a "successful business woman" because women are now expected (and expect themselves) to be proficient in both areas at once. And single women, young and old, are not immune to rising expectations and other societal pressures.[2]

Stevenson and Wolfers's explanation is scandalous because it seems to fly in the face of what feminism has taught us over the last forty years: that more opportunities and freedom for women would automatically correspond to increasing levels of happiness for all. At the same time, their explanation is poignant because it underscores the challenge contemporary women face every single day: the intense pressure of piecing together the spheres of work and home in a way that honors the integrity of both. In the face of such huge expectations, women inevitably fail to achieve all that they set out to accomplish and, in turn, thwart their own general happiness and satisfaction with their lives.

So how can women, particularly female Christian leaders, respond to this tension? How can we effectively coalesce the various pieces of our fragmented identities—mother, worker, wife, single person, Christian? How can we bolster our level of happiness without continuously compromising anyone else's (be it in the home or the workplace)? In this chapter, we'll discuss three ways female leaders have shouldered the varied aspects of their full lives.

EXPECT LESS

First, *expect less.* Expecting less of ourselves and of the situations life presents to us seems counterintuitive, especially given Western society's entrenched attitudes about expecting more.

Paul and I refer to the first decade of our marriage—his thirties, my twenties—as the California Years. In many ways, we had the time of our lives. We lived in a two-bedroom parsonage on the campus of Cornerstone Bible Church, a church built in the 1930s with rocks drawn from the quarries in the neighboring San Gabriel Mountains. The little house had no insulation, no dishwasher, no laundry, and no central heating or air conditioning, but we hardly missed them. (Okay, summer scorchers were brutal, especially during the rolling blackouts, and I constantly envied those with laundry machines.)

We spent a lot of time on the mountain trails just outside our back door, often covering forty to fifty miles a week. On Friday nights, we would camp out in the local Barnes and Noble, talking with locals and reading until midnight. We were not gamblers, but we took trips to Las Vegas to hike the desert in every season, hang out on the Boulevard, or just stand, mesmerized, while the pastry chefs at Jean Philippe Patisserie in the Bellagio expertly flipped crepes. On Sundays after church, we would dig our toes deep in the sand on Laguna Beach and watch the sun set.

It was an age of adventure, but it was also, for me, an age of anxiety. I had grown up hearing that women could have it all—work, home, marriage, family—but until the California Years, I had never stopped to think about how that would actually work. I guess I just thought that one day, everything would slip into place. I knew God had called me to go to seminary, but I also felt the pressure of the proverbial ticking clock. I had expected to be able to do it all, never mind the fact I had never actually *seen* anyone do it all. *What if I can't finish my degree? What if I have to drop out because I get pregnant, like that other woman did? What if it's so hard that it takes me too long to complete it—far past the years to have kids? What will I do if I do get it in time and have kids? Who will care for them?* For someone who usually has a clear idea of where she is headed, the hard light of reality cast a deep, crisp shadow over my vision of the future.

Carrie, a high school director at a local church, had a similar experience after the birth of her first child. "Even before we had kids," she remembers, "balancing ministry and personal life was a huge issue. In ministry, the need is constant. I'd get to work early to check emails because more interruptions come later in the day—like people hurting and needing care. Then I'd study for a message for a few hours, meet with leaders, then spend time with kids for six to eight hours."

After the birth of her daughter, things became even more complicated. "My brain is someplace else. I feel like I'm always running back and forth. My daughter is usually with my mom [when I'm at church]. There's so much to do in so little time, so the interruption factor is really brutal. After I had my daughter, I dropped down to thirty-two hours a week. So I cram in planning and scheduling in the morning, then I pick up my daughter and I meet with people in the car while Sophia is in the back seat, napping. I feel like I'm making stuff up as I go."

Married women are not the only ones who expect a lot of themselves. Susan, a middle manager in a Christian nonprofit, says, "The temptation for the single woman is to overwork. It's very easy to do more than what's required, especially if it's a profession related to the ministry."

One woman who serves overseas says the problem of overflowing expectations is not just an American one. "One of the main challenges has been balancing my family and ministry. My children are generally well adjusted because we talk and take time to be away with them. But it is a trouble to balance—I leave by 7:30 a.m. and that is early! You know how it is ... time is the thing. We don't have time to do everything. Somehow we've got to make it work."

Single or married, American or African, women expect a lot of themselves in most areas of their lives. Before I became a work-at–home mom, each week I would analyze my time according to six different roles: spiritual, physical, home, wife, mother, and ministry/work. For each role, I set several goals I wanted to achieve that week and planned how I was going to achieve them. Inevitably, I would set the bar too high and then feel guilty for all I did not accomplish. But I am not alone. Let's look at what is expected of women in each of those areas.

SPIRITUAL

Recently the Barna Group released a study that revealed that most women are either "mostly" or "completely" satisfied with their personal spiritual development. Likewise, most women say they have either an "extremely close" or a "pretty close" relationship to God. On first blush, it seems that I really am alone in feeling like I do not always measure up spiritually and my relationship with God can seem distant at times. Here is the catch though: Barna's study was exclusively self-report, and thus subject to something called "the problem of self-report."[3]

The problem with self-report is that there is no way to know if the people surveyed are actually telling the truth unless you use some external means of validation. And how could we verify each person's spiritual development, let alone their relationship with God? It is not that people are outright lying; often they either give "the right answer" in order to be viewed favorably by others or they report things as they wish they would be, not as they actually are. David Kinnaman, president of the Barna Group, writes, "In many ways, women's self-perception revealed in this study seems to be aspirational. Women want to be influenced by the Bible, but they reject the idea of being heavily affected by the media. So these aspirations may be reflected in the numbers. Still, the way women describe themselves reveals something: they seem to know how they want to be *perceived* by others."[4] All of that to say, I am not completely convinced that most women are satisfied with their spiritual growth or their relationship with God.

PHYSICAL

Research indicates that over 80 percent of women over the age of eighteen do not like what they see in the mirror.[5] This statistic is probably skewed toward Caucasian women since black and Asian women tend to have more positive self-esteem. We have learned our bodies, as they are, are not enough, and we have learned it young. In a study conducted at the University of Central Florida, researchers found that half of girls ages three to six already worried about being fat, and a third wanted to change something about their body.[6]

HOME

Greater responsibility for the finances does not mean less responsibility at home. According to the annual Time Use Survey, women spend 2.6 hours a day on household chores compared to 2.1 hours a day for men. The same study showed that 83 percent of women and 65 percent of men spent time each day doing household chores. Despite spending more time than men on household chores, 68 percent of women still identify an unclean house as a source of guilt.[7]

MARRIAGE

Marriage may be the one area where women do not place such great expectations on themselves. According to the Barna Group study cited earlier, only 2 percent of Christian women said that their most important goal in life is to enhance their marriage. In fact, marriage is listed below several other goals, including health (6%), career (5%), lifestyle (4%), personal growth (4%), morality (4%) and financial objectives (3%). The researchers suggest this may be due to the fact that most Christian women (59%) report being satisfied with their marriage.[8] This comports well with what I have heard female leaders express. When asked who has been their primary support, more often than not, women cite their husbands.

PARENTING

When asked what their most important role in life is, the overwhelming majority of women (62%) cite being a mother or a parent. Being a follower of Christ ranked a far second (13%).[9] The priority that women place on being mothers elevates all the more the tension they feel in regard to their work and ministry life. When female leaders become mothers, they often have to make difficult choices because their desire to be home with their children (if financially feasible) is strong.

Some women rely on full-time help through caregivers or family members while they continue working. If they have a flexible working environment (such as a pastoral position), many women choose to press on in their positions, integrating the children creatively into their work. They bring children along while mentoring or doing visitations and hire part-time help for times when they need to be in the office. Some women step away from their leadership positions for a few years while their children are young, returning to ministry once their children are in grade school. Other women leave indefinitely.

WORK

Women now hold more than half of all jobs in the United States and slightly more than half of all managerial positions, though men are more predominant in upper management positions. Whether single and living alone, single with children, or married and out-earning their partner, the majority of women now report being the primary breadwinner of their home, whether they like it or not. This does not mean that women are earning more; rather it is largely due to a sluggish economy and the fact that 40 percent of the women surveyed were either single or divorced—making them the sole provider of their family. Regardless, the majority of women now shoulder the bulk of the financial responsibility for their household.[10]

Women expect themselves to perform well in each of these areas, and when we do not measure up, it is natural to feel guilty and dissatisfied with our lives. It is not enough simply to balance; we desire to excel. It is true that the demands on our lives are great, but we do not have to make it more difficult by placing unrealistic expectations on ourselves. By curbing our expectations for what we can simultaneously accomplish in life, ministry, work, and family, we are more prepared to celebrate our successes than dwell on our failures.

I used to think that reducing my expectations for myself was taking the easy way out; that if I did not meet my goals, something was wrong with me. (Who am I kidding? I still think that sometimes.) I did not want to accept that something was wrong with my expectations. As a result, I often did not feel content with my life or myself. I would think, "Once I'm done with this degree ..." or "Once my house is clean ..." or "Once I lose ten pounds, then I'll be content." But contentment never came because I kept pushing myself further, refusing to acknowledge my finiteness.

True contentment is related not to the absence of desire or difficulty but to the ability to be satisfied with whatever circumstances life presents to us. In Philippians 4:11–13, the apostle Paul writes, "I am not saying this because I am in need, for I have learned to be content whatever the circumstances. I know what it is to be in need, and I know what it is to have plenty. I have learned the secret of being content in any and every situation, whether well fed or hungry, whether living in plenty or in want. I can do all this through him who gives me strength" (NIV).

Regardless of his outward circumstances, Paul had learned that the secret of contentment consisted of modifying his expectations to meet current reality and trusting in God and his provision. For women, true contentment and happiness will only come if we accept our circumstances and do the best we can in those circumstances—and no more. If you are putting a lot of time into work or young children, it may mean you cannot teach the fall Bible study. If you are working and still manage to make it to your kids' soccer game or gymnastics competition, it may mean your house is a mess. It's okay. Be kind to yourself.

RESIST COMPARISONS

Scarlett O'Hara was the belle of the South and had her pick among all the men in the surrounding counties—all, that is, except Ashley Wilkes, the very one she imagined herself to be in love with. Ashley married Melanie, a mild-mannered, gracious woman who understood him better than Scarlett. Throughout *Gone with the Wind*, Margaret Mitchell's staggering Civil War novel, almost every decision Scarlett makes is out of envy. She marries Melanie's brother to make Ashley jealous; she goes to Atlanta ostensibly to care for Melanie but really to win Ashley's affections; she gives Ashley a job at Tara and later at her lumber mill. It is only after Melanie's death that Scarlett realizes that, all along, she had only imagined her love for Ashley. Scarlett's envy drives her decisions and blinds her to the blessings in her own life. Ultimately, she loses the love of the one man she truly loved, Rhett Butler.

Envy is the enemy of contentment, and it's born in the act of comparing ourselves with others. Saint Augustine defined envy as "dissatisfaction with our place in God's order of creation, manifested in begrudging his gifts and vocations to others."[11] Philosophy professor Rebecca Konyndyk DeYoung puts it this way: "Envy is feeling bitter when others have it better."[12] In church tradition, envy is one of the seven deadly sins, the parent of jealousy ("offense at the talents, success, or good fortune of others"), malice ("ill will, false accusations, slander, backbiting"), and contempt ("scorn of another's virtue, ability, shortcomings, or failings").

Biblical writers exhort believers to stop comparing themselves to one another and find contentment in what they have been given. "Keep your life free from love of money, and be content with what you have," writes the author of Hebrews (13:5). Luke recounts the words of Jesus, "Take care, and be on your guard against all covetousness" (Luke 12:15). The apostle Paul tells us, "Only let each person lead the life that the Lord has assigned to him, and to which God has called him" (1 Cor. 7:17), reminding us elsewhere that "there is great gain in godliness with contentment" (1 Tim. 6:6 RSV). To truly find contentment in our present circumstances, we must resist the temptation to compare ourselves with others, because that is where the root of envy lies.

Often, we think of material goods or physical features as the only ways of comparing ourselves to another. We think that if we keep ourselves from envying our neighbor's house, car, husband, or body, we are safe. But that is not the case. Like the envy we see between Cain and Abel (Gen. 4:2–5), Jacob and Esau (chapters 25–27), Rachel and Leah (30:1), Joseph and his brothers (37:8), the urge to compare *ourselves* with others is strong, especially when it comes to the spheres of family and our vocation. As my friend author Caryn Dahlstrand Rivadeneira told me, "I've found the biggest trigger of my own mommy guilt is comparison. The second I stop focusing on the mom and woman God created me to be and start measuring myself against other moms (and women), it leaves all sorts of room for guilt. All I see are the ways I don't measure up to others. I forget to see all the ways I excel—in line with my gifts and experience and calling."

For women, comparisons with others can be especially bitter. Single women compare themselves with married women and married women compare themselves with single women. Stay-at-home moms compare themselves with working moms, working moms compare themselves with stay-at-home moms, "hybrid moms" compare themselves with both, and women who want to be mothers compare themselves with everyone. And each group thinks that another has it easier or better. Yet the act of comparing ourselves with others is ultimately deceiving because no matter how much we think we know others, we never have full access to how God is (or is not) working in another person's life.

Take, for example, King Solomon. Of all the figures in the biblical narrative, the most obvious person to incite envy is King Solomon. In the early days of his reign, it would have been difficult not to envy him. Under his reign, the people were happy, satiated, and safe (1 Kings 4:20, 25). Solomon was not only a successful king but also a scientist, carefully observing the natural world. His wisdom exceeded that of all the people of the East (4:30–31), amazing even the Queen of Sheba (10:8). But his joyful kingdom and great wisdom were nothing compared to his wealth. Every year he received twenty-five tons of gold, not including the taxes he garnered from traders and merchants. His throne was made of ivory and pure gold, and all the drinking cups and food utensils were made from pure gold. He had four thousand stalls for his chariots and his twelve thousand horses. He was the envy of many, and many came from far and wide to receive his counsel.

And yet from the beginning of King Solomon's tale, the biblical writers allude to the double-mindedness of his heart and what would eventually become of him. Though the law expressly forbids kings from amassing wealth, that's exactly what Solomon does. He takes hundreds of foreign wives and allows them to worship other gods. He spends almost twice the amount of time building his own house than he does building the temple of the Lord.

Then, the unthinkable: Solomon turns away from the Lord, worshiping other gods, building high places for the gods of his wives (1 Kings 11:7). His kingdom is torn away from him. The Scriptures say, "So Solomon did what was evil in the sight of the LORD and did not wholly follow the LORD, as David his father had done" (11:6). Contrast Solomon with the example of another: Jesus of Nazareth. In the very midst of striving for opportunities and advancement, most Christians say they want to be like Jesus, a dusty-footed itinerant preacher born in a stable, without a home or physical heir, who never wrote a single sentence, was killed by one of the most horrid and shameful methods known to humanity, and was buried in a borrowed grave in what was viewed, at the time, as one of the most inconsequential places in the world.

At least, that's what it looks like this side of heaven. He had hardly the kind of life one would envy. But in and through the life of this less-than-enviable character, God was building a kingdom. Indeed, this less-than-enviable character *was* God, living and working redemptively among us. And so when we envy, we are only measuring what the Lord has given us compared to *what we perceive* he has given others.

It may be that right now you are frustrated with the season of life you are in. For me, transitioning from working full-time to being a stay-at-home mom was a huge adjustment. From the time I was very young, I have defined myself according to my work, a place where I have always found meaning and deep satisfaction. So when there was no "job," I struggled deeply with my shifting identity because I felt so irrelevant, hidden in obscurity.

Maybe life just is not turning out the way you thought it would. Maybe you are in a lonely place and feel of very little use to God or others. Maybe your pain is so great you cannot see how God could be working. Maybe that is why it is so easy to compare your life and your achievements to others.

If so, rest in the assurance that God is working. Moses worked for forty years in obscurity on the back side of the desert before he was called to lead the Israelites out of Egypt. David tended sheep in the lonely pastures around Bethlehem before shepherding the people of Israel. By resisting the urge to compare ourselves to others, we make room to celebrate not only the ways that God is working in our lives but also the way that God is working in the lives of others.

GET CREATIVE

Folded in the bottom of the oak armoire my husband and I received as a wedding gift from my parents is an assortment of handmade afghans and quilts. I watched my mother sit in our living room on countless evenings and knit those afghans, and I remember thinking on more than one occasion that I wanted my life to be like them — neat, color-coordinated, and perfectly looped.

Yet in my life as a wife, a mother, an academician, and a writer, I have realized that life is not anything like an afghan and is, rather, more like the crazy quilts my grandmother made — humble, brave, uneven, and messy. Sometimes the pieces do not always fit together seamlessly. Sometimes they are a little ratty and frayed at the ends. So it is with our lives as women in contemporary society. As *Time* magazine reporter Nancy Gibbs writes, "If there is anything like consensus on an issue as basic as how we live our lives as men and women, as lovers, as parents, partners, it's that getting the pieces of modern life to fit together is hard enough; something has to bend." To really, truly release ourselves from these great expectations and find true contentment, we have to get creative in the way we piece together the varied aspects of our lives.

First, realize and accept that life is messy and that having to fit the pieces together is the reality for the vast majority of us. Accept that life is far more like a crazy quilt than an afghan. Jodie Niznik, pastor to women at Irving Bible Church, makes things work because her employer has allowed her a very flexible schedule. "I do a lot of work from home," she says. "My boss allows me to make sure my family is a priority. No one ever questions it if I have to leave at 2:30 in the afternoon to be sure my daughter makes it to her piano lessons." On Bible study nights, while her kids are at church or with her husband, Jodie teaches late into the night. Her schedule is not eight to five, cut and dried. There is a flow to things.

Second, set your priorities in piecing things together. When Judith Shoemaker's sons were young, she took positions in ministry that fit their schedule, like being part of the youth ministry leadership team. When they became teenagers, they just went to work with her. "I was afraid they wouldn't like going to church because they were with their mom, but enough people invested in them that they weren't just with their mom. They were involved in a lot of the work I did. I've got a good relationship with both of them today." As they grew older, she took on more responsibilities, eventually becoming the co-pastor of their church. "When they were older, they understood when I needed to go to the hospital to visit someone. They knew the person and knew I had to go."

"One thing I tell young women," Judith says, "is that they have time. There's plenty of time. Your kids always come first—no one else is called to be your kids' mom. Take a long view of things—they'll grow up, and there will be plenty of years ahead. People watch that, and it shows people what it means to lay down your life and sacrifice for your kids."

Kit Danley founded Neighborhood Ministries, a holistic outreach center that ministers to low-income families and at-risk children, when her own children were very young. "I played hide the ministry from my kids. Because I wanted them to have a normal life. Now, we were raising our kids in inner-city Phoenix where there were no white people—hard to hide. I wanted to have normal 'mom' time with no interruptions. If you asked my kids, 'Did your mom hide the ministry?' they'd laugh. My kids had a mostly normal childhood." Kit counsels many young women who come to Neighborhood Ministries to serve. "I say to those women who are going to get married and have kids, 'Okay, your life is going to get more complicated, but it's not the end of the day. Your calling doesn't stop once you get married and have kids.'"

Third, accept help from others. As I mentioned earlier, almost every married leader I have spoken with has expressed how important their spouse's support was to their success as a leader. When Jan Paron went back to seminary to get a PhD in missiology from Fuller Theological Seminary, her husband worked nights while she worked days and split the household chores. When Alexandra Armstrong, host of *Scriptureology* on Christian Television Network, was asked if she could start a television program on Bible study, she says, "I laughed. My husband did not laugh. He always says I don't get enough attention."

When Dale Fincher realized that there was not a place for his wife, Jonalyn, to serve alongside him at the ministry he worked for, he resigned. "They had no interest in us working together as a husband-wife team," she remembers. "So he resigned so we could work as a team. That's how Soulation started." Donna Jones, vice president of Living Media at Insight for Living, said that she could not do her work without the support of her husband. "He is a wonderful man, and it's very kind of him to support me in my calling. He has to sacrifice when I'm traveling for work, so when I'm off, I'm off. I try to be respectful of him since he is my number one priority."

If you do not have a spouse (or happen to have one who is not helpful), reach out to friends, family members, and your local church. Many female leaders have been able to build a support network with people from these communities.

Finally, enjoy the uniqueness and unpredictability of your crazy quilt. Releasing ourselves from the illusion that everything will fall neatly into place if only we try harder, if only we push a little further, gives us the freedom to more fully appreciate our lives as they are—a bold, beautiful patchwork of love and work.

CONCLUSION

Both the importance of women's leadership in religion, industry, commerce, and politics and the importance of building a stable home should be celebrated and esteemed, for women's involvement in each of these areas brings with it a certain fullness and richness. As a new mom and an academic, seeking how to merge these two spheres in ways that honor both, I find something in me resonates with Stevenson and Wolfers's assessment that women's rising expectations for themselves largely account for the decline in their happiness. Despite my daughter's giggles and my sighs of relief at her finally getting enough food and rest, despite moments of deep satisfaction and well-being, I could not shake the nagging burden of my own self-created to-do list. I wondered where all my time had gone. I wondered how on earth I was going to finish a dissertation while raising a young family, even with shared household duties. Rather than savoring the moment, I let my expectations get ahold of me, my emotions, and how I assessed what a "successful" weekend alone with my daughter looked like.

It's not that I think I cannot be a mother and a professional; it's just that it's probably more realistic for me to realize that I cannot be "all things to all people excellently all at once." So even though the balance and perfection of the afghan life appeals to me in a deeply profound way, I want to be wise enough to release my great expectations to embrace, wholeheartedly and without reserve, the crazy-quilt life: humble, brave, uneven, and sometimes, yes, quite messy.

Understanding our calling and managing our expectations are foundational to navigating successfully our way to places of influence. In the next chapter, we will look at the first of several obstacles women face in our work or ministry context: the double bind. Can a woman be likable and still be a leader?

CHAPTER 6
IRON LADIES

ARE YOU *a* GOOD LEADER *or a* GOOD WOMAN?

To wear your heart on your sleeve isn't a very good plan; you should wear it inside, where it functions best.

—Margaret Thatcher

Levelland, Texas, is a small island of municipality in a brown ocean of cotton fields. The dusty town, located up on the Caprock, was commemorated by Robert Earle Keen in his song "Levelland": "Flatter than a tabletop, / makes you wonder why they stopped here, / wagon must have lost a wheel or they lacked ambition one." Even as a little girl, I wondered that very thing—nothing but earth and sky, brown and blue, no shelter from the sun's rays from dawn to dusk.

My grandmother Barbara was born in a small two-bedroom house just outside of Levelland in 1932, at the height of the Great Depression. Listening to her stories is a lot like listening to Laura Ingalls Wilder describe her life in *The Little House on the Prairie.* "We were poor," she says, "but we never knew it. Everybody was poor."

Before the onset of every winter, all the neighbors would get together to kill the hogs they raised on the farm. A single hog provided food for my grandmother's family of five all winter. My great-grandmother Gladys cured the ham with salt and brown sugar and stored it in the smokehouse. She cleaned out the intestines and made sausage, and made lard for cooking. At meals, they paired the meat with canned vegetables from their summer garden.

In the summer, they had chicken and fresh garden vegetables. Every morning, Gladys walked out to the henhouse, picked up a chicken by the neck, and whipped it in a tight circle like a rope, breaking its neck. They often took their meals out to the pasture of mesquite, cacti, and small grasses where the cows grazed, and had picnics.

Gladys made her three daughters dresses out of chicken feed sacks, which in those days came in printed floral patterns. One year, my grandmother's younger sister burned down that two-bedroom house playing with matches, and so they lived in the dirt-floor garage for seven months while their house was rebuilt. When the sands came in the time of the Dust Bowl, they hid in the dugout—a cellarlike hole in the ground covered with wood—that my great-grandfather had made to live in when he first broke the land for farming cotton.

I suppose it is that honest, unaffected background that is largely responsible for my grandmother's resilient, unflappable spirit. In many ways she is the anchor of our family. If I had one word to describe her, it would be *steady.* In all my life, I have seen her cry twice: once at the time of my grandfather's death and another during a particularly charged family conflict. Once, when I complimented her on her strength, she casually shrugged and said, "Sometimes you just have to be tough."

But being tough, as least in her case, never made her any less a lady. She still, to this day (at eighty years of age), dresses better than I do. She is not afraid to get dirty digging in her garden, but she is religious about getting her hair and nails done. She manages to be both firm and feminine, forthright and warm, confident and kind. She manages to be, all at once, a good leader and a good woman. When I think of an "iron lady," I think of her.

But she is an anomaly. One of the biggest challenges for women is gender stereotyping based on our perceptions about what makes a good leader and a good woman. People hold certain ideas about what characteristics they perceive to be good in women, men, and leaders, and the qualities we desire and expect of women are at odds with the qualities we desire in leaders.

When women display the desirable leadership traits — confident, competent, assertive, and bold — they cease to be viewed as warm and caring and instead are perceived as tough, aggressive, and domineering. This creates a double bind, because if women act in ways consistent with gender stereotypes, they are not viewed as competent leaders, but if they act in ways consistent with good leaders, they are not liked. In political circles, these women are called "iron ladies."

Whether we realize it or not, we do not think a woman can be both a good woman and a good leader. This discrepancy (called "role congruity theory of prejudice") between our perceptions about good women and good leaders presents a sizable challenge for female leaders to navigate in order to serve well within their communities.

Our perceptions are important aspects of reality. Although we see dimly, as through a mirror, we do still see, and what we see is important in our decision-making process. If we do not perceive women to have the raw materials to be a good leader, we are less likely to select women for leadership positions. Perceptions, even stereotypes, are not inherently bad; the function of stereotypes is to provide us with a framework so our minds are better equipped to handle the large amounts of information we receive on a daily basis.

Consider this scenario: you happen upon a neighborhood with trash on the sidewalks, litter in the streets, graffiti on the walls next to the sidewalks, broken windows in the homes, and bars on every door. In a second, you realize that this may not be a safe neighborhood. So you proceed more cautiously. This is a stereotype in classic form: it gives you information regarding a present reality based on previous experience. Stereotypes become bad or negative when they are incorrect or uninformed and when entering a new cultural context.

Role congruity theory has been studied the world over since the 1970s, but only once has it been studied in Christian organizations.[1] In my study of twenty-one Christian ministries, I found some interesting things about the double bind and Christian women.

It is important to point out two things. First, I specifically studied perceptions about female leaders serving in Christian parachurch ministries, not evangelical churches. Therefore, to be as accurate as possible when describing the findings, many of my comments in the next two chapters are directed to women serving in those contexts. Having said that, I am fairly confident that much in both chapters will resonate with female church leaders, because many have expressed similar experiences and frustrations through the interviews and conversations I have had with them over the years.

Second, these results relate to perceptions, not to how things are in reality. So when I say, for example, that women are perceived to have less analytical ability, or, in the shorter form, that women have less analytical ability, I am always referring to perceptions about women. I do not believe this is how women actually are; this is how we perceive them. The discrepancy between what we think of Christian women and who they actually are is the very thing that makes the task of leadership more difficult for Christian women.

In this chapter, we will take a close look at what I found, how it impacts Christian women, and what individuals, communities, and ministries can do to help women serve well.

THE BACKSTORY: A BRIEF HISTORY OF THE DOUBLE BIND

Hillary Clinton has never been especially liked, and her flinty demeanor has won few hearts. When her husband began campaigning for the presidency in 1992, she was relatively unknown, but by the time of his inauguration in January 1993, about 50 percent of the American public viewed her favorably. As she took a more active role than her predecessors in affecting public policy, her favorability rating plummeted, only to catapult to a new high of 60 percent when her husband was impeached.

The graph of Hillary's favorability ratings looks like the tracks of the Magic Mountain roller coaster at Six Flags. But a curious thing happens when you match the graph to a timeline of events: when Hillary is succeeding, people like her less, not more. Her favorability tumbled when she announced her intention to run for senate and again when she ran for president. When she cried on the presidential campaign trail, her likability spiked, and ever since she lost the presidential nomination, her likability has slowly increased. And that, in a nutshell, is the double bind, the catch-22 for all female leaders: to succeed, you need to be liked, and to be liked, you need to temper your success.

With rare exceptions, such as Cleopatra, the Queen of Sheba, Catherine the Great of Russia, Queen Elizabeth I, and Queen Mary, for most of human history, men, rather than women, have occupied leadership positions in government, business, and the home. But in the last fifty years, women have made significant strides in improving their position in societies. In the United States, where it was once "considered unseemly for a woman to vote, or even to assert her right to vote, women now constitute over half of the electorate and occupy many of the nation's highest offices."[2]

From Benazir Bhutto, former prime minister of Pakistan; to Margaret Thatcher, former prime minister of Great Britain; to German chancellor Angela Merkel; to former US secretaries of state Condoleezza Rice and Hillary Clinton; to Indira Gandhi, third prime minister of India, women have enjoyed increased access to top leadership positions around the world, in both the political sphere and the business world.

And yet, as we have seen in earlier chapters, women are still underrepresented in both the public and private sectors, especially when it comes to upper levels of leadership. In an effort to figure out what might be keeping women from those upper levels, for the last forty years researchers have sought to determine if stereotypes about women, leaders, and leadership hinder would-be female leaders. Since men have been leaders for the bulk of human history, do we naturally penalize women because our ideas about good leadership are inherently masculine?

In the early 1970s, an organizational psychologist named Virginia Schein conducted a groundbreaking study about gender-role stereotyping and characteristics people thought were necessary for successful leadership. In her landmark study, she developed an innovative list of ninety-two adjectives commonly used to describe different character traits, like *aggressive, ambitious, creative, fair, understanding, decisive*, and *consistent*.

Each participant received the same ninety-two-item list, but directions were modified for different groups. One group was asked to rate, on a scale of 1 to 5, how true each characteristic was of a successful leader, while other groups were asked how true the characteristics were for "women in general" and "men in general." When she compiled the results, Schein compared how people described successful leaders with how they described "women in general" and "men in general." Schein found that male and female participants perceived successful managers as possessing characteristics that were more commonly associated with men than with women.

Over the last thirty-five years, Schein's Descriptive Index has been replicated throughout various times and contexts, resulting in an abundance of research on gender-role stereotyping and characteristics needed for successful leadership. In every context and culture studied, from 1970 until today, the double bind is one of the most significant hindrances for female leaders. When female leaders talk about the struggles they have faced as leaders, the double bind is more often mentioned than any other single issue.

I wondered, though, if women serving in Christian contexts would have the same level of difficulty with this issue. Would our Christian orientation impact what kind of leaders we desired? Would we value the "softer" leadership characteristics—like communal, relational, and transformational traits—a bit more than the secular world because of our faith? If so, would women then not be associated more consistently with the ideal leader?

THE DOUBLE BIND FOR CHRISTIAN WOMEN: THE STUDY

In my study, I used a modified version of the Schein Descriptive Index to survey 424 people serving in twenty-one parachurch organizations affiliated with the Christian Leadership Alliance. I included ministries of all types: publishing, outreach, evangelism, humanitarian, and discipleship ministries. For each type of ministry, I included organizations of all sizes. As with Schein's study, each person was given the same set of character traits and was asked to rate how true those character traits were of a particular group of people.

Some people were asked to rate how true each of the traits was for "successful leaders," while others were asked to rate them for successful male managers, successful female managers, male managers, female managers, women in general, and men in general. When the surveys were complete, I compared what character traits people associated with successful leaders with how people associated the traits with the other groups. Were successful leaders and men thought to have the same traits? What about women? Did they differ, and if so, how?

Predictably, women differed significantly from successful leaders in every way possible. To get a clear idea of how they differed, let's look at each set of characteristics.

COMMUNAL

Communal characteristics include being aware of others' feelings, being helpful, kind, passive, submissive, and sympathetic. Communal characteristics are tremendously important for any society, and it is these traits that lead women to careers in nursing or teaching. The warmth that undergirds these characteristics provides the basic building blocks for relationships and ensures that individual members of a community are cared for. And yet they do not scream "leader," which is why these communal characteristics are not typically valued in work settings. When a group of researchers from Rice University analyzed recommendation letters for a faculty position, they found that the more a woman was described in communal terms, the less likely she was to be hired.[3]

As is the case in secular organizations, people working in Christian parachurch ministries perceived women to be more communal than successful leaders.

AGENTIC

Agentic characteristics include aggressiveness, ambition, assertiveness, analytical ability, and self-confidence—traits that are more commonly associated with men. *Agency* is related to a person's capacity to make choices and take action; the term originates in the medieval Latin word *agentia*, which means "doing." Agentic characteristics are often negatively associated with communal characteristics, meaning that if a person has agentic characteristics, they do not have communal characteristics, and vice versa.

As is the case in secular organizations, people working in Christian ministries perceived women to be less agentic than successful leaders. Women were perceived to be less aggressive, ambitious, assertive, dominant, forceful, and self-confident, and to have less analytical ability than successful leaders.

TASK-ORIENTED

Task-oriented characteristics include competence, competitiveness, decisiveness, independence, intelligence, skilled in business matters, and speedy recovery (meaning the ability to get over setbacks or offenses quickly). People with task-oriented characteristics are focused and committed to achieving the key objectives and goals of a strategic plan. In a similar way to that of agentic-versus-communal traits, task-oriented characteristics have often been negatively associated with relationship- or people-oriented characteristics. In this study, women were perceived to have significantly fewer task-oriented traits than successful leaders.

RELATIONSHIP-ORIENTED

One of the more surprising things I found is that people in Christian ministries do not think women have as many relationship-oriented traits as successful leaders. This goes against previous research, because historically, women have outscored successful leaders on traits such as compassion, cooperation, tactfulness, and understanding.

It is possible that relational tension and competitiveness among women could explain these results, but further research is needed to be certain.

TRANSFORMATIONAL

Transformational leadership characteristics include traits such as attending to others' needs, considerate, encouraging, inspiring, optimistic, supportive, and trustworthy. In recent years, popular leadership books have emphasized "the female advantage" in leadership.[4] With our growing preference for transformational and authentic leaders, experts have suggested that women now have the edge over men because women are typically perceived to demonstrate transformational leadership traits naturally. Not so among people serving

in Christian parachurch organizations, because women were perceived to have fewer transformational leadership traits than successful leaders.

These results are troubling, but not surprising, because they are
consistent with the bulk of previous research: as is the case in secular
organizations, the double bind is an issue for female leaders serving
in Christian ministries. What was surprising is this: when I compared what people thought of female leaders with what they thought
of successful leaders, there were very few differences. People thought
female leaders were more agentic and less transformational than successful leaders, but even these differences were small.

In previous research, female leaders were more similar to successful leaders than women in general, but not as similar to successful
leaders as male leaders were. However, in this study, people thought
female leaders are more similar to the successful, ideal leader than
both men in general and male leaders. It could be that Christians
have a stronger preference for leaders who have "softer" leadership
skills—such as the communal and relational qualities typically associated with women—because of our faith and the pastoral climate
we expect in a Christian environment.

Further, since female leaders were so similar to successful leaders,
when you directly compare how people described women in general
and how they described female leaders, you get two drastically different descriptions.

WHAT THIS MEANS FOR CHRISTIAN WOMEN

Since the double bind is an issue for women serving in Christian
ministries, this means that women face what researchers Alice Eagly
and Steven Karau describe as "two forms of prejudice": (1) women
are less likely to be perceived as potential leaders because leadership
ability is more stereotypical of men, and (2) the leadership behavior

of female leaders will be perceived as less favorable because it violates the prescribed gender role.[5]

Here is what each of these forms of prejudice means for Christian women. In chapter 2, we discussed how our expectations govern what we see. If we do not perceive women as having leadership ability, then women will have less access to leadership roles because fewer women will be identified as potential leaders. Without proactive strategies that are designed to identify and develop future female leaders, the leadership pipeline will likely run dry.

Second, since female leaders violate their prescribed gender roles by demonstrating more task-oriented and agentic traits, they will be viewed less favorably than male leaders, and their progress and success as leaders will be hindered. This is the problem Hillary Clinton has: she demonstrates appropriate leadership traits, but she is not especially likable. The same behavior we identify as assertive in male leaders is viewed as brusque or bossy in female leaders.

Both forms of prejudice mean that women serving in Christian ministries face more obstacles than men on the path to successful leadership.

Further, since perceptions of female leaders strongly correlate with perceptions of successful leaders, but greatly contrast with perceptions of women in general, it means that Christians view female leaders as exceptions to the rule. This creates a false dichotomy between women in general and female leaders. As Sarah Sumner notes in her book *Men and Women in the Church*, "In the evangelical community, gifted Christian women are labeled as 'exceptional' because they are anomalies to the paradigm."[6] In the next chapter, we will discuss the ramifications of this dynamic in-depth.

NAVIGATING THE DOUBLE BIND

So what is the way forward? What can be done about these challenges?

The double bind can be counteracted on both the individual and organizational level.

INDIVIDUALS

On an individual level, female leaders can learn to say things in a way that will be heard. This means avoiding the extremes of being an aggressive communicator and speaking too softly or crying while you are speaking. Shortly after I began working at Azusa Pacific University, we had a faculty meeting to discuss a marketing strategy to get freshmen to use the university libraries. During the meeting, a colleague presented a plan he had been working on for several months. I knew the plan would not effectively reach the generation coming in, and I told him so in a matter-of-fact way. I did not really think there was anything specifically aggressive in the way I said it, so I was surprised to see tears well up in his eyes over my criticism.

I thought about that moment for a long time afterward and realized that my style of communicating was a bit harsh coming from a woman, and a young woman at that. But how can you tell the difference between an assertive style and an aggressive one? Elisa Morgan, President Emerita of MOPS and founder of *FullFill* magazine, believes it is rooted in the leader's goal. "Aggressive leaders fight for their turf to win," she says. "Assertive leaders express their position and opinion in order to advance the body of Christ."

Tami Heim, the CEO of the Christian Leadership Alliance, recommends that women adopt an approach called "the velvet brick approach," a blend of "strong decision and compassion. It requires a leader to have a healthy heart, a heart that's really centered on who you are, what you've been called to do, and the people who are within that calling. Tough news is tough news ... but the strength of your decision and the way you communicate it comes from a deep-seated belief that you're doing the right thing, not from the fact that you're the boss."

Since there is a strong preference for leaders to have relational, communal, and leadership qualities, it's possible for female leaders to receive more positive evaluations of their leadership style, especially if they utilize a more relational and transformational leadership style. This is important, since, as we saw before, female leaders are perceived to be more agentic but less transformational than successful leaders.

CHURCHES AND ORGANIZATIONS

In addition to changes on an individual level, ministries can strategically help women navigate the double bind in a variety of ways.

Select women for leadership positions. Given that both men and women prefer a more relationally based, transformational leadership style, a style that is often adopted by women, key decision-makers in the hiring process can be open to selecting women to fill more leadership positions in their organizations. According to my study, female managers are perceived to be more similar to successful leaders than male managers. This, along with the desire for a more relational, transformational leader—a style women usually adopt—indicates that there should be a growing openness to female leaders in Christian ministries.

When I asked a group of women serving in Christian ministry what they thought was the biggest barrier for them, they identified "the absence of a female role model" as the top barrier and also reported that ministries were doing only a "fair" job of ensuring there were enough women in the pipeline. Proactively selecting female leaders will mitigate the challenge posed by this barrier.

Develop female staff. If ministries can't find skilled women to promote, they could consider developing female staff through leadership and mentorship programs. Forty percent of the women serving in ministry reported that their organization had no leadership programs to help develop female leaders. Ministries can create and implement training programs or workshops to enhance individual staff members' understanding of effective, desired leadership traits (i.e., relational, transformational leadership) as well as improve their ability to exercise those traits in their own leadership roles and organizational contexts.

Mentoring programs help younger women or newer employees connect with more seasoned leaders on staff. Mentors can help women identify areas of giftedness and provide a vision of how God can work through their lives by using their gifts. Mentoring programs also help younger leaders understand how to integrate ministry and family life effectively.

Further, ministries could create a climate that eases the tensions between work and family life that burden women, especially single mothers. This would include a performance evaluation system that neutralizes the impact of family leaves or obligations and eases the transition before, during, and after maternity leaves.

Increase the visibility of female leaders. This can be accomplished by providing ample opportunities for women of all generations to display their talents, competencies, and accomplishments. Senior leadership should strive to assume responsibility for promoting the advancement of female leaders by ensuring that key decision-makers are open to recruiting more women for leadership positions. Since women who seek opportunities for themselves are often seen as overly aggressive, it is especially important that opportunities be provided through sponsors or mentors.

Educate staff on gender issues. Ministries can bolster awareness of issues regarding gender and leadership roles by providing more educational opportunities to increase staff members' awareness of perceptions regarding gender and leadership and their practical significance in their ministry. These educational opportunities could be followed up with organizational initiatives that move the ministry toward a more gender-balanced leadership structure, such as ensuring the presence of more female leaders in executive leadership positions within the organization. These educational opportunities could take the form of companywide retreats, training sessions, or even online training programs to be conducted by each staff member.

Addressing the issue of gender stereotyping and perceptions about ideal leaders is necessary in order for women to navigate effectively the pathways into higher-level leadership positions. In doing this, Christian ministries will ensure that *all* leadership talent, both men and women, within their organization is effectively utilized and deployed for the advancement of their mission and vision.

Encourage growth. Ministries can more fully tap into the pool of resources available to them by becoming more intentional about discovering and utilizing the giftedness of individual female staff members through staff development programs. All too often, Christian ministries provide spiritual gifts inventories but fail to follow through on how those spiritual gifts can be used within the organization. Another way to help individuals understand their spiritual gifts is by connecting them with a pastor or spiritual director.

Individual believers have the responsibility to steward their gifts well, to use them effectively to build up and equip the church. Women do not have a *right* to be a leader so much as they have a *duty* to steward their giftedness. Likewise, communities of believers have a responsibility to ensure that individuals are free to exercise the gifts distributed by the Holy Spirit, unencumbered by obstacles or impediments in whatever form they may take.

The ability for solid, godly leadership is not bestowed solely upon the shoulders of a single gender. All members of the body of Christ—regardless of age, gender, or ethnicity—have a role, a part to play in the ministry of the church. Paul describes the body, the bride of Christ, working together, "the whole body, being fitted and held together by what every joint supplies, according to the proper working of each individual part" (Eph. 4:16 NASB).

CONCLUSION

My grandmother was not the first iron lady, and neither was Margaret Thatcher. Tucked into the tales of religious apostasy in the book of Judges is the story of another iron lady, a woman who was able to faithfully navigate the roles of wife, prophetess, and judge. Deborah, whose name means "honeybee," served the nation of Israel as a civil leader in the dark and difficult times of the judges. "In those days," writes the author of Judges, "there was no king in Israel. Everyone did what was right in his own eyes" (Judg. 21:25).

Enchanted with the urban, cosmopolitan lifestyle of the Canaanites, Israel was constantly turning its back on God and worshiping the gods of the Canaanites. As a result, they suffered under the reign of Jaban, king of Canaan, until Deborah, "a mother in Israel," came along. In her role as a prophetess, she spoke to the nation on behalf of God, assessing their behavior in light of God's laws. In her role as judge, Deborah settled disputes and controversies. She was a formidable military commander, and her victory against the Canaanites secured forty years of peace for the Israelites.

Contrary to our perceptions, Christian women are—and can be—effective leaders. By carrying out the initiatives outlined in this chapter to counteract these perceptions, individuals and ministries can effectively steward the giftedness God has given women.

In the next chapter, we will examine the dichotomy between how we perceive the average woman and how we perceive female leaders.

CHAPTER 7
SUPERWOMEN

EXPOSING *the* MYTH *of the* EXCEPTIONAL WOMAN

The most common way people give up their power is by thinking they don't have any.

—Alice Walker

From 1939 to 1945, more than 130,000 women and children from more than twenty nations passed through Ravensbrück, the notorious concentration camp built especially for women by Heinrich Himmler in 1938. Ravensbrück was a labor camp, and prisoners, regardless of health or age, were forced into hard labor building rockets, weapons, munitions, and explosives for the Nazis. Many women died from starvation, torture, slave labor, medical experiments, and the gas chambers. Corrie and Betsie ten Boom were sent to Ravensbrück in September of 1944 for harboring Jews in their hometown of Haarlem, Holland. At great personal risk, Corrie had become the ringleader of the underground network that provided safety for hundreds of Jews.

Of Ravensbrück, she wrote, "Barracks 8 was in the quarantine compound. Next to us—perhaps as a deliberate warning to new-comers—were located the punishment barracks. From there, all day long and often into the night, came the sounds of hell itself. They were the sounds not of anger or of any human emotion but of a cru-elty altogether detached: blows landing in regular rhythm, screams keeping pace. We would stand in our ten-deep ranks with our hands trembling at our sides, longing to jam them against our ears, to make the sounds stop."[1] But these horrors did not deter the ten Boom sisters. They held Bible studies and worship each night in their bar-racks. Betsie died at the camp in December of 1944, just twelve days before Corrie was released due to a clerical error. Ravensbrück was liberated four months later.

For her actions, the state of Israel named Corrie ten Boom "Righ-teous of the Nations," an honorific title for those who risked their lives for Jews during the Holocaust. Corrie was knighted by the Queen of the Netherlands, and to this day, visitors from around the world tour Corrie's home to see "the hiding place."

If the term *Superwoman* should be applied to anybody, it most cer-tainly should be to Corrie ten Boom. And yet Corrie was a remarkably ordinary woman. I do not mean to say that she did not demonstrate extraordinary faith in extraordinary times, because she certainly did. I mean that if you look at her life from this side of heaven, you see a very ordinary woman whom God used in an extraordinary way.

Daughter of a Dutch watchmaker, unmarried, childless, and middle-aged by the time the war came, Corrie lived with her aging father and her unmarried sister, Betsie. She ran the business side of her father's watch and clock shop while her father did repairs and Betsie took care of the house. Every evening after supper, they read the Scriptures together as a family. A simple life. Ordinary.

THE TROUBLE WITH EXTRAORDINARY

Recently, *Fast Company* identified an interconnected group of sixty female executives, entrepreneurs, artists, government officials, philanthropists, and academics who are "formulating groundbreaking initiatives and hacking long-outdated aid models by tapping new thinking and a growing data set that suggests that investing in girls and women will create measurable economic benefits for all."[2] These women, whom *Fast Company* calls the "League of Extraordinary Women," are using their influence and fiscal muscle to provide financial opportunities for the world's poorest women and young girls.

The statistics are grim. One in three women throughout the world—a total of one billion—will be raped or beaten at some point in their lives. The proportion of women exposed to physical violence in their lifetimes ranges from 12 percent in China to 59 percent in Zambia. In several countries, the number of women aged fifteen to forty-nine who have been subjected to female mutilation is extremely high—so high that in some countries, such as Guinea, Egypt, and Eritrea, the number reaches to 100 percent.

Many women are caught in cycles of poverty that span generations, but through the empowerment of microfinance loans, they are able to make choices that will minimize the risk of violence in their lives. Through microfinance loans, instead of being forced into early marriages in exchange for financial security, young women can gain the economic stability they need to support their families and transform their communities.

While I am glad that women like Maria Eitel, the CEO of Nike, are advocates for women around the globe, I am concerned about how *Fast Company* describes these women as "extraordinary." The trouble with labeling some women extraordinary—even women as successful as *Fast Company*'s group of sixty—is that it simultaneously diminishes the achievements of many other, less visible women and disempowers still others by making it seem as though advocacy and other philanthropic endeavors are only for extraordinary women.

In the last chapter, we discussed that perceptions of female leaders strongly correlate with perceptions of successful leaders, but greatly contrast with perceptions of women-in-general, creating what I think is a false dichotomy between the average woman and female leaders. In this chapter, we will explore how this false dichotomy impacts Christian women.

As I pointed out at the beginning of the last chapter, in order to be as accurate as possible when describing the research, many of my comments are directed to women serving in Christian parachurch organizations, though there is reason to believe much of what is said will be applicable to women serving in local churches.

Second, this research is about perceptions, not about actual reality. When I describe female leaders as "superwomen," I do so not because I believe they are superior in some way to the average woman but rather because this is how we perceive them—we think they are anomalies, exceptions to the paradigm.

This is the problem I address in this chapter. Distinguishing some Christian women as exceptional or extraordinary widens the gulf between women—between the women who are impacting the world in big ways and the women who one day could—or the women who influence the world in much smaller ways. The Scriptures are clear that God does not call extraordinary people; he calls ordinary people to accomplish extraordinary things.

THE MYTH OF THE EXCEPTIONAL WOMAN

On her first day in union construction, Susan Eisenberger was sent to a bank in downtown Boston to help a journeyman pull wires. When she got to the work site, the guard denied her entrance, not believing she was a construction worker. Women's liberation had granted women access to all fields—even construction—but women were still few and far between. "The myth that *no* women were capable of skilled trades was replaced by the Myth of the Exceptional Woman,"

Eisenberger writes, "the disconnection of any successful woman from the rest of her gender."[3]

The same dynamic is taking place in Christian churches and organizations. The myth that *no* Christian women can lead has given way to the myth that only exceptional or extraordinary women can lead. As a result, we have entered a permanent phase of pioneering, in which women continue to be met with significant structural and organizational challenges.

The myth of the exceptional woman has negative ramifications for female Christian leaders, for would-be leaders, and for Christian organizations. Do not get me wrong; each woman is unique, and God's mission for each of us is unrepeatable. But we need to be careful not to conflate "unique" with "exceptional." And the trouble is not even really with the idea of exceptionality but with what it is we call "exceptional." What do we mean when we call someone an exceptional woman?

We say that Mozart was an exceptional composer and that Ernest Hemingway was an exceptional author, but that Jane Austen was an exceptional *female* author and that Margaret Thatcher was an exceptional *female* prime minister. When it comes to women, our exceptionality is often associated with our gender, not our gifts. Only in those areas traditionally associated with women, such as teaching kids or nursing, do we identify the skill, not the gender, as exceptional. We might very likely call a female nurse "an exceptional nurse." It is almost as if we are surprised when a woman's gifting falls outside of traditionally accepted roles.

This might sound like a trivial objection or frivolous hair splitting, but if we continue to view female Christian leaders as exceptions among women rather than exceptional leaders, we will continue to be stuck in the pioneering phase, our progress small and unremarkable. If there is a difference between Christian women who lead and Christian women who do not, between Christian women who lead entire organizations and Christian women who lead small, at-home

Bible studies, we need to discern clearly the nature of that difference. Let's look at four potential areas where women can differ.

DIFFERENCE IN NATURAL TALENTS

Are some women *born* exceptional leaders? The question reminds me of the character Remy in Pixar's *Ratatouille*. Remy is a rat with the heart of a chef. When his pack are forced to flee their home, Remy is separated from them and winds up in the sewers of Paris. Eventually, Remy finds himself cooking in Paris's finest restaurant for Paris's toughest critic, Anton Ego. When Anton tastes Remy's food and discovers the identity of the chef, he writes in his review, "Not everyone can be a great artist, but great artists *can* come from *anywhere*."

Despite his humble origin, Remy was *born* a talented chef.

In the movie *Amadeus*, the composer Antonio Salieri discovered this as he read the first—and only—draft of Mozart's Symphony No. 29 in A Major. "He was simply writing down music already finished in his head ... like he was taking dictation. I was staring through the cage of those meticulous ink strokes at an absolute beauty." Salieri knew that the very best of his talent and hard work could not compete with what came easily, naturally, to Mozart.

Is the genius of a successful leader the same as the genius of a poet, a composer, or an artist? Maybe. I think there are some things about great leaders that just boil down to *soul*—like charisma, that mysterious ability to win the affection and attention of others. Some say that charisma can be learned, but I have my doubts.

Sometimes, when my daughter Ellie is not looking, I watch her play with her friends. She fascinates me because on one hand, she is so like me—a little blonde, blue-eyed mini-me—with the same mannerisms, the same furrowed brow of compassion. She is so *familiar*, but then she is also so incredibly *other*, so very different from me. She is animated, enthusiastic, energetic, and has a certain warmth about her. Kids flock to her like people gravitate to a bright patch of sunlight on a cold day. In any group, it is not long before she takes the reins.

I did not teach her that. She was born that way. At the very most, I have taught her about the importance of kindness and created a safe place for her to be authentically herself. So maybe the genius of a successful leader is not exactly like the genius of a poet, but there is something, some innate quality that distinguishes highly successful leaders. Even so, that does not excuse those of us with more modest leadership gifts from using them to the very best of our ability. Salieri, too, though not a musical genius, was a great, prestigious composer whose music blessed many.

And yet researchers say that the great bulk of leadership—a full two-thirds—is learned, not genetic. Most of the raw materials for leadership are drawn from the pool of our environment. Leadership, for the most part, is born in the crucible of our experiences—our religious experiences, what our parents and siblings taught us, our education and training, our peers and mentors.

So it may be that there are Christian women leading who are exceptionally gifted, but it does not necessarily follow that they are all born with it. The danger in boiling the difference down to genetics is that it makes leadership seem unattainable, an exercise in futility. It's like when girls are "reminded" right before a test that boys are naturally better at math. When they're not "reminded," they score better. Our core, inmost beliefs shape our expectations of what we can and cannot achieve.

DIFFERENCE IN SPIRITUAL GIFTING

While natural talents are gifts that are not necessarily employed for spiritual purposes and do not depend on the empowerment of the Holy Spirit, the spiritual gifts are and do.

I had been at APU for less than a semester when I found myself riding along with Sarah Sumner to a speaking engagement in downtown LA. I was floored by the depth of her knowledge and by her captivating teaching style. She taught for five hours with no notes. I had just started my master's degree, but I thought to myself, "There's no way I could do that. I might as well hang my hat up now."

I had done this before. Back in college, I was so staggered by C. S. Lewis's *Till We Have Faces* that I, the writing major, barely wrote a single word for another six years. Why even try in the face of such "competition"? I was wrong. The giftedness of Sarah Sumner and C. S. Lewis did not excuse me from using the giftedness God had given me any more than the giftedness of a popular Bible teacher excuses other women from teaching Scripture.

The Corinthian church dealt with this very thing. Some of the Corinthians were so focused on the spectacular gifts that others with less flashy gifts wondered if they had a place in the body of Christ. To them, the apostle Paul said, "Now there are varieties of gifts, but the same Spirit ... it is the same God who empowers them all in everyone. To each is given the manifestation of the Spirit for the common good.... All these are empowered by one and the same Spirit, who apportions to each one individually as he wills. For just as the body is one and has many members, and all the members of the body, though many, are one body, so it is with Christ" (1 Cor. 12:4, 6–7, 11–12). This laser-beam focus on the spectacular gifts is rooted not in humility, as you might think, but in pride. Bowing out of ministry because some gifts are more apparent—or because your gifting does not seem to be on the same level as that of others you know and admire—is rooted in the paradox of insecure pride, the habit of being dissatisfied with ourselves for what we cannot do.

Both being satisfied with ourselves because of spiritual gifts and being dissatisfied with ourselves because of our possible lack are rooted in pride, from which we need to turn and repent. In that place of repentance, we will discover how wonderful it is that we do not have to be great. How wonderful it is that I do not have to write a heartbreaking work of staggering genius in order for God to work beautifully through my little life.

Biblical scholar Gordon Fee writes, "In Christ, all have drunk deeply of the Spirit and have been enriched with every kind of spiritual gift. But such gifts must be forever humbling, for they lead finally to a discipleship that goes the way of the cross, not the way of false triumphalism."[4] The abundance of gifts that some Christian leaders display does not excuse us from serving the Lord with all he has given us.

Every Christmas, the stirring lyrics of Katherine Kennicott Davis's "The Carol of the Drum" bowl me over. The lyrics relate the story of a poor young drummer boy who was summoned to the nativity by the magi, who had brought the finest, most expensive gifts in the ancient world: gold, frankincense, and myrrh.

When summoned, the poor drummer boy reflects, "I have no gifts to bring . . . to lay before the King." But this drummer boy was courageous and he offered all he had. "I played my best for him . . . and he smiled at me." May we all have that same courage to offer up to the Lord all we are and not be deterred because our gifts may not glitter as gold. They may, after all, win us the smile of the High King of Heaven.

DIFFERENCE IN PREPARATION

A. W. Tozer once wrote that the most important thing about a person is what that person thinks about God. What he meant is that the whole of our lives — our character, our thoughts, our relationships, our worship, and our ministry to others — flows from our theology, from *who it is* we believe God to be. "We tend by a secret law of the soul," he writes, "to move toward our mental image of God. This is true not only of the individual, but of the company of Christians that composes the Church."[5]

That is why theological education is so important for leaders. It's not because anyone needs another plaque on the wall or some kind of bragging rights; it's because the people of God, especially leaders, need the education and theological training to, as Dostoevsky writes, "increase tenfold their strength to serve the very truth and the very deed they loved and set out to accomplish."[6]

And yet fewer Christians — and even fewer female Christians — go to seminary to deepen their understanding of God. They have their reasons for not going, often good ones. Some do not go because they cannot afford to; others because they are burdened with the responsibilities of family and work; others because they know that the chances are slim they actually will be hired in a position that requires seminary training; and still others because no one has cast a vision for how important seminary is for those called to the work of ministry.

With so few people willing or able to go to seminary, it is incumbent upon the church to train and equip leaders for the work of ministry. In fact, that's what the Lord told his people to do: to *go* and to *teach*. But somewhere along the way we lost the vision for why teaching is so important. Maybe it was when we started equating Christian education with crayons and kids' crafts. Maybe it was when we started focusing the ministry of our churches on the unchurched, and thought we would leave the deeper training to seminaries. Maybe we lost it a long time ago, back in 1925 in a Tennessee courtroom during the Scopes trial.

Christian women may differ because some have had more preparation—whether through seminary, work experiences, or family experiences. It is true that female Christian leaders need other types of training and education than what is provided by seminaries and Christian education programs in the local church, but it is also true that education that is Christian, when executed well, is the foundation for all other training. In the next chapter, we will look closely at how Christian women are—or are not—being prepared for ministry leadership in local churches.

DIFFERENCE IN OPPORTUNITY

The final way Christian women can differ involves a difference in opportunity. This may or may not be related to a difference in training. A woman could go to seminary and receive all the appropriate degrees for ministry and still not be able to find a position in a local church. A woman with all the appropriate training and expertise could still be overlooked at her church. The women leading today, especially women in upper levels of leadership, have often come into their positions from the business world, where there are fewer impediments to their development as leaders. How many Christian women would have the foresight to enter the business world with the goal of becoming a leader, eventually, in a Christian ministry?

But there are other gaps in opportunity. There are certain limitations for women serving in complementarian contexts. Some women's lives are packed full of family life and secular employment. There are limitations due to economic and social issues: Does a Hispanic woman living in South Central Los Angeles have the same opportunities as a woman living in Pasadena? Hardly. What a whole world of difference those sixteen miles make! In chapter 9, we will look deeper at the various limitations women face in opportunity and how they can (and cannot) be addressed.

These are four areas of potential difference between Christian women that might lead to differences in levels of leadership. Regardless, it is not because some women are ontologically superior or worthier in ways that cannot be bridged through education, skill development, and opportunities for professional growth and development.

If individuals and churches and Christian nonprofits want to close the gap between what we think of female leaders and what we think of women in general, these are areas for targeted reform. Begin by busting the myths surrounding what it takes to be a leader, by clarifying the roles of natural and spiritual gifting, and by examining differences in training and opportunity and finding strategic ways to offset those differences.

SUPERWOMEN (IT'S NOT EASY)

In September of 2000, American singer-songwriter John Ondrasik, under the stage name Five for Fighting, released the song "Superman (It's Not Easy)." In the comics and movies, Superman is viewed from the pedestal we have put him on—unmovable, unbreakable, untouchable. But in this song, Ondrasik gives Superman a voice, revealing how Superman feels up there on his pedestal: lonely and emotionally vulnerable.

The gap between how others perceive Superman and how he perceives himself is great; he doesn't feel as strong and competent as people think he is. While trying to live up to everyone's expectations, alone he shoulders the full weight of his loneliness and the fragility of his emotional life — his doubts, personal pain, and homesickness. Is there anyone to whom he can show his real face?

Though released in 2000, "Superman (It's Not Easy)" shot to popularity after the events of September 11, 2001 — all the way up to thirty-eight on the Hot 100 charts on October 27, 2001. The song was adopted by rescue workers and emergency workers to ease the burden of their work among the rubble of the Twin Towers. Media stations intercut the song along with film footage of the attacks, and Ondrasik performed the 9/11 anthem at the Concert for New York City that winter.

Though perhaps without the same level of gravitas as for the 9/11 emergency workers, the song "Superman" relates the same sort of struggle that many female Christian leaders may grapple with at one time or another because they are so few and the expectations of them are so great.

I was sitting with a woman I'll call Morgan at a Café Brazil in Addison, Texas. Morgan was a prominent, well-respected Christian leader whose business acumen and leadership ability sent her straight to the top levels of leadership in her organization. She had achieved a great deal in her career and had received recognition and several awards for her work. But when we met over coffee and BLTs, it wasn't the awards or achievements she spoke of; it was the loneliness of leadership.

"You know, I feel as if I have to be twice as good as a man," she said as her eyes filled with tears. "More than that, I have to be perfect. All my decisions are scrutinized so heavily that I can't afford to be wrong about anything. It's exhausting to keep up this front ... and lonely."

My mind tried to process the contrast before me: from the "super-woman" whose tenacity and unbreakable spirit were known far and wide to the human, broken and bleeding, sitting in front of me.

The trouble with the myth of the exceptional woman, for female leaders, is similar to the struggle I've heard my male students discuss. As pastors, they feel as though they need to have every aspect of their lives together for their congregation, to be a worthy role model. Who can maintain a façade of perfection and invincibility? For how long? With their crammed schedules, they have no time to look outside their congregations or organizations for peers or mentors to help them shoulder the great burden of responsibility, leaving them isolated and alone on the sure path to burnout.

WOULD-BE FEMALE LEADERS

From the time I was eighteen until my twenty-first birthday, it seemed I couldn't stay sober for more than a few hours. The wounds from an abusive parent, a broken home, and a broken heart were just too painful to handle with the wide, clear eyes of sobriety. But I knew my life needed to change. I wanted a better life and to be a better person. So in the early morning hours of my twenty-first birthday, I watched the cold February rain drizzle down the wind-shield, and I decided to get sober.

It wasn't a miraculous, instantaneous change. There were relapses and doubts as I faced my emotions. The numbness that alcohol offered wore off. This "new life" felt like second skin, and I often felt like an outsider, like I didn't fit in with my peers at church, all of whom were young seminarians studying for a life of ministry leadership. I, too, wanted to be used by God, to be a leader who impacted the lives of others for good, but I was haunted by the thought that I would never be like those seminary students; there was too much water under the bridge. They had never done the things I had done, and nothing, not even a death on a cross, would make me forget that.

The things I had done would always, always be true of me. And who in their right mind would want a leader like Halee, the misfit of many mistakes, when they could have Marissa, the one who had loved God from her youth and had never strayed too far from the sidewalk? The chasm between my peers and me was great. Who could overcome it? It wasn't until much later that I understood that these people, though they didn't have a history like mine, were still flawed and imperfect.

The myth of the exceptional woman has created a similar chasm between women who lead and would-be female leaders. The expectations are so high that some women fail to recognize similarities between themselves and successful female leaders. They doubt they can meet such high expectations and determine that leadership is not God's plan for them.

In her article "Why Millennial Women Don't Want to Lead," Julie Zeilinger argues that though women today don't face the same "*Mad Men*–esque type of sexism" that prohibited women from leading in the past, they face much subtler forms of sexism. She writes, "The truth is many young women today fail to lead because of the pressure put on young women to be perfect and moreover the disparity in what we teach our sons as opposed to our daughters ... women equate leadership with perfection in a way that men don't. Men are generally taught that perfection is not a necessary component of success, that, in fact, they can fail miserably—even commit felonies—and still bounce back to power."[7]

In her book *Perfect Girls, Starving Daughters*, Courtney Martin argues that young women today were told that they could be anything, but instead heard they had to be everything.[8] Like the Photoshopped images of thin, beautiful women that stare at us from the pages of every magazine, the myth of the exceptional woman magnifies our imperfections and keeps us from even wanting to aspire to leadership.

"In order for women to lead—for women to want to lead," Zeilinger comments, "... it's essential that we question and change a society that sets the standard for achievement impossibly high for women and upsettingly low for men."

LEAGUE OF ORDINARY CHRISTIAN WOMEN

How then do we overcome the myth of the exceptional woman and bridge the divide between Christian women who lead and Christian women who would? How can we build a league of "ordinary" Christian women whom God is using in extraordinary ways? There are several things that can be done on organizational and individual levels to help more women navigate the paths to leadership. On an organizational level, many of the suggestions posed in the last chapter will address this issue, including implementing leadership development programs, establishing mentoring and sponsoring relationships, raising awareness of gender issues, and raising the visibility of female leaders.

On an individual level, if you are a woman looking for greater areas of influence, here are a few strategies to help you develop as a leader. (Men can also employ these strategies to encourage their development.)

1. *Gain an awareness of your natural talents.* If you are not sure what your natural talents are, enlist a group of friends to help you unpack what it is you seem to do well without even trying. You can also do an "energy analysis": What activities fill you up and what drains you? What activities put you in a state of "flow" where you enjoy them so much you lose track of time? Lean into those strengths, focus on them, and use them often — daily, if possible.

2. *Gain an awareness of your spiritual gifts and how you could use them.* You can complete a spiritual gifts inventory for a general idea, but it is also helpful to connect with a pastor or spiritual director to help you process where God is calling you to use your gifts.

3. *Get the appropriate training.* Seminary training is especially important for women who would like to serve in church contexts. More and more seminaries are offering evening courses and courses you can take online. If you cannot afford seminary, exercise the self-discipline to educate yourself in

theology, biblical studies, and ministry. For theology, begin with broader, comprehensive theological books such as Millard Erickson's *Christian Theology*,[9] Wayne Grudem's *Systematic Theology: An Introduction to Biblical Doctrine*,[10] or *Integrative Theology* by Gordon Lewis and Bruce Demarest.[11] For biblical studies, learn how to practice proper hermeneutics by reading books like *Grasping God's Word* by J. Scott Duvall and J. Daniel Hays.[12] Then do your own studies of God's Word using the tools they introduce you to. If your church offers courses, take them. For ministry practice, Michael Anthony's book *Foundations of Ministry* is a good place to start.[13] Attending conferences on an annual basis is another way to expand your knowledge and your networks.

4. *Build a network of strategic, spiritually beneficial relationships.* If you don't have a mentor, seek one out. Find a woman who is doing what you feel called to do and connect with her. Connect with peers who share your passion for ministry and accountability partners who will challenge you to grow as a leader. Look for a sponsor in your church or organization who can connect you with more leadership opportunities.

5. *Learn to become an optimist.* Train yourself to view difficult situations as opportunities for growth rather than impediments. What is possible? What can God be working for good in this organization or situation? How can I look at this more positively?

CONCLUSION

In *The Great Divorce*, C. S. Lewis describes a parade of "Bright People" who have come from heaven to greet those who have come from hell. Among them, Lewis sees one so beautiful, so extraordinary that he assumes her to be Mary or another of the saints. Lewis writes, "I cannot now remember whether she was naked or clothed ... if she were clothed, then the illusion of nakedness is doubtless due to the clarity with which her inmost spirit shone through her clothes ... but I have forgotten. And only partly do I remember the unbearable beauty of her face. 'Is it?... Is it?' I whispered to my guide. 'Not at all. It's someone ye have never heard of. Her name was Sarah Smith and she lived on Golders Green ... Aye. She is one of the great ones.' "[14] Sarah Smith—an ordinary woman with an ordinary name who lived in an ordinary section of London—and yet in the eyes of God, she was one of the "great ones."

You know too the kind of people the Lord chose when he began his earthly ministry. Fishermen. Tax collectors. Ordinary. That's the way the Lord is. He uses ordinary people in extraordinary ways. From Corrie ten Boom to St. Therese of Lisieux (a French Carmelite nun of humble origins who is now recognized as a revered saint), ordinary people have been used by God in amazing ways. My prayer is that God would help us all to be as "ordinary" as Sarah Smith of Golders Green.

But what do we *really* expect God can do through women today? Do the educational programs at our local church line up with what we say we believe? Do we really believe that women can be Christian leaders? If so, how are we preparing them for that role? That is the subject of the next chapter.

CHAPTER 8
BRAVE NEW WOMEN

MINISTRY *by* CHRISTIAN WOMEN

Of the women, by the women, but for humanity.

Frances Willard, *The Autobiography of the American Woman*

My short-term memory can be fuzzy these days due to several concussions I received from various misadventures in my teenage years, but the weekend of September 4, 2005, is as clear as glass. All week long, the images from the devastation caused by Hurricane Katrina came rolling in. By Sunday I was overwhelmed with grief for the people of New Orleans. What could be done for these people? How could I help them from Los Angeles? Paul and I went to church that morning anxious to hear how we, as a community, would be helping victims of Hurricane Katrina.

As usual, when we arrived at church, booths for various church ministries were already set up outside in the milky sunshine of a California morning. I approached the woman manning the women's ministry table and asked, "Do you know if there are plans to help the victims of Hurricane Katrina?" Confusion furrowed her brow and wrinkled her nose. "No, I'm just here to talk about the women's retreat," she said as she reached down for the pink and brown pamphlet, her blouse shifting downward as she moved, scooping far below an appropriate level, even for Southern California.

"It's our annual Spa Sisters retreat. It's still a few months away, but it's only $400 for two nights at a spa in San Diego. Of course, at that price you have to share a room, and it doesn't include the treatments—all the facials, massages, hair, and nail appointments are extra. But you know, it's gonna be great. There's no official teaching time, but it's what us women need most of all, right? We're all so stressed we need a little pampering, a little gossip time, a little bit of girl time. You know what I mean."

Now, I try to be a good Christian, but remember what I said earlier about my being a tell-it-like-it-is truth-teller? That gets me in trouble sometimes. I stared at her silently, hurricane-force winds blowing through me. Really? A $400 spa weekend is what women need most of all? Images from New Orleans flooded my brain, and more. The Hispanic single mother who attended our church and who could barely afford to keep gas in the car and food on the table for her five kids. The broke and spiritually hungry college students. How would they afford something like this, and how could we justify raising money for scholarships in the face of such graver needs?

Really? Yes, women are stressed with the demands of very full lives, but a spa retreat is not what they need most of all. What they need most of all is to know the love of God and have the opportunity to communicate that love to people who need to hear it— like the prostitutes working the streets just thirty miles away on the corners of Hollywood Boulevard. Women would be better served pooling that money and taking a weekend trip to serve the poor in downtown LA. Spa Sisters, indeed.

In the end, I surprised myself. With a Herculean effort, I managed a smile, took the pamphlet, and walked away. But I have never forgotten that moment, and there have been far too many similar moments for me to remain silent on the state of women's ministries in many of our local churches.

On one occasion, while I was in seminary, I was paired with a lay leader to build a women's ministry from the ground up. But from the first meeting, it was clear we didn't see eye to eye. She thought women were suffering and needed lighthearted weekly teas and craft parties; I thought women were suffering and needed to know how to read and interpret the Word so they would know how to invite God into their suffering. She thought they needed to know how to make their homes comfortable and inviting; I thought they needed a theological framework through which they could contextualize their pain. Our visions could not have been more different.

Unfortunately, these experiences aren't anomalies. Tea parties, crafts, and women's socials are far too common. We have Spa Sisters and luncheons and crafts and baby clothes sales, but we don't always have good theology or good biblical teaching. We often don't practice good hermeneutics. But thankfully, more women are beginning to question the limited vision set forth by many women's ministries around the country. Author and speaker Carolyn Custis James laments the fact that "so many Christian women believe it's possible to subsist on an anorexic spiritual diet."[1] Far too many women's ministries do not offer up the kind of robust teaching that nourishes our deepest hunger and helps women become strong, biblically minded leaders who are ready to take action in their communities.

A few years ago, Amy Simpson at *Christianity Today* wrote a blog post titled "Why I Don't Do Women's Ministry." Her piece was the most popular blog article that year. Since then many more women have voiced a concern about contemporary women's ministries.

In this chapter, I will explain why I think these critiques make a substantive point, that they are not just making mountains of mole-hills. If you drive down to the root of the issue, it's easy to see that the problem is not just a matter of difference in taste or preference; it is a philosophical and cultural difference. Let's begin by looking at the history of women's ministry in the local church.

THE CRADLE OF MINISTRY TO WOMEN: A HISTORY

French aristocrat and political writer Alexis de Tocqueville came to America in 1831, back when America was just a toddler trying out her legs. He suspected that democracy would soon sweep over all of Europe, and in order to better know what was coming, he sailed to America to study democracy in its infancy. De Tocqueville thought that to really understand a man or a nation, it is not enough to study them when they are full-grown; you must go back to the cradle. He writes, "We must watch the infant in its mother's arms; we must see the first images which the external world casts upon the dark mirror of his mind; the first occurrences which he witnesses; we must hear the first words which awaken the sleeping powers of thought, and stand by his earliest efforts, if we would understand the prejudices, the habits, and the passions which will rule his life. The entire man is, so to speak, to be seen in the cradle of the child."[2] I believe that principle is also true on the organizational level. To truly understand an organization, a program, or just a way of doing things, you have to go back to the beginning. If we want to understand the usual way of doing women's ministry, we need to understand its history. When, where, and for whom did it begin?

Many individual churches and denominations describe the history of women's ministries as ministry *by* Christian women, not *to* Christian women. In the nineteenth century, Christian women were the pioneers of social reform, working to alleviate human suffering by striving to eliminate various social ills and injustices, including slavery, lack of women's rights, alcoholism, illiteracy, crime, and poverty.

Christian women in the Northeast planted US bases for the Young Women's Christian Association, an organization founded in the United Kingdom to help young women who had no family to support them. The Grimke sisters were southern-born abolitionists who traveled around churches in the North, speaking out against slavery and urging other southern Christian women to oppose slavery. American Quaker Lucretia Mott's passion for global human equality began at a boarding school in Millbrook, New York, when she found out male teachers were paid three times more than female teachers. She became a minister and was the only woman to speak at the organizational meeting for the American Anti-Slavery Society in Philadelphia.

Frances Willard was the driving force behind the women's temperance movement, becoming a longtime president of the Women's Temperance Christian Union. Quaker Mary Ann McClintock was an organizer for the first women's convention, which was spearheaded by Elizabeth Cady Stanton and held at a Wesleyan Church in Seneca Falls, New York, in July of 1848.

These are just a few of the many stories of brave Christian women buried in the annals of church history, but they are enough to illustrate the fact that the cradle of women's ministry was ministry *by* Christian women. At some point, though, ministry by Christian women became ministry *to* Christian women, but this shift is largely undocumented. One reliable source points to the societal upheaval of the 1960s and 1970s as the period in which an interest in ministering to Christian women developed. Theology professor Patricia Chapman writes, "It was a period when seminaries training young men for ministry opened their doors to young women for ministry as well. They were exploring and experimenting with new ideas, new ways to meet the needs of various components of their congregations. It seemed an appropriate time to look at how to develop a ministry to women."[3] From there, the ministry of the church to adults fragmented into gender-specific ministries.

Ministry to women may have begun as a way to equip women with a knowledge of Scripture, but what we have today in many churches is a ministry that is characterized by superficiality and the most extreme traits of stereotypical femininity. Men's ministry, geared toward sports, man-caves, and hunting, is no better. Separated from one another, both male and female gender-specific ministries have become distorted caricatures of real-life, flesh-and-blood men and women. It's not that men and women aren't different, because they are. But separating the genders makes us less than, not more than, real men and women. Maybe that is partly why these ministries feel so artificial. This in itself is serious, but my greatest concern about the current women's ministry paradigm is its flawed philosophical foundation and cultural indifference.

Please do not misunderstand me. I have the greatest respect for women who have devoted their lives to caring for the souls of women. My purpose in this chapter is not to critique their endeavors but to show why this specific approach to women's ministry is not working for all women. As one women's ministry director told me, "The programs I have had to drop [due to low attendance] are those for younger women. It's hard to know how to appeal [to younger women]. If you come up with any ideas for how to deal with it, I'd love to hear them." I believe the women leading traditional women's ministries have the very best of intentions, and my goal is to help them develop more effective ministries.

WHAT IS THE PURPOSE OF TRADITIONAL WOMEN'S MINISTRY?

Behind every educational system, teacher, or curriculum is an ideology, a philosophy—a set of beliefs about the world, human nature, and how people learn. It might sound impossible to decipher an unstated philosophy of education—even your own—but it is actually not that difficult. You can usually get to the heart of it by asking a few questions:

1. What are the foundational truths or beliefs driving the educational process or ministry? What is the purpose of human life? How do you live a good life?
2. Who are the students and what are they like?
3. What kinds of knowledge, skills, or attitudes are necessary to live a good life?
4. How do you acquire that body of knowledge, that set of skills, or those attitudes?
5. What specific educational practices are used to cultivate these things among students?

With these questions in mind, let's look at an example I think fairly represents the stereotypical women's ministry. Not all women's ministries are like this, but stereotypes are stereotypes for a reason; it means that ministries like these are predominant enough that they are the first thing that springs to many people's minds when they hear the term *women's ministries*.

My example comes from a church in middle America I'll call Crestview. It is located in a relatively small community in the suburbs of two larger metropolises. A predominantly white community (93%), only 30 percent of all households are married couples, while 57 percent are single women. Crestview's women's ministry states that its two ultimate goals are to help women become what God wants them to be and to provide support and encouragement through Christ-centered relationships. From that statement, we can infer that a Christlike character and Christian relationships are the "ultimate" truths or goods.

Neither fulfilling the Great Commission (the going out and discipling) nor caring for the impoverished (part of what the apostle James called "pure and undefiled religion in the sight of our God" [James 1:27 NASB]) is explicitly mentioned, but Crestview's women might include those things as part of a Christlike character. To find out more, one needs to look at the curriculum, events, and activities.

There is one Bible study that meets twice a week, once on

Thursday nights and once on Friday mornings. There are periodic retreats for escape. For outreach, they host Out with the Ladies, relaxing, entertaining evenings with cake exchanges, card games, and movies. There are two special events held during the year: a Ladies' Thanksgiving Brunch and a Ladies' Fellow-sip Tea held to "[give thanks for] being a girl." They have an ongoing outreach ministry team—a group of nail beauticians, hair stylists, and masseuses who go to a battered women's shelter and other local churches.

First, to achieve a Christlike character, they rely on one Bible study, two social events, and two ongoing "outreach" activities, both of which are geared toward relaxation. We can look at this several ways. The goal of "becoming what God wants us to be" is vague—how will they know if they have achieved it? Even if they do have a clear concept, how would character be developed with one Bible study and a sprinkling of social events? In a community with so many single females, I appreciate the emphasis on relationships. I can also appreciate the outreach ministry team to the extent that it is a ministry of positive touch to women who have been abused, but I wonder if these types of outreach events are sufficient to draw women—especially unbelievers—into a deep relationship with God.

The thing that concerns me most of all is the underlying view of women. While they say their goal is Christlike character, their events—even their vocabulary—reveal that they believe, like the woman at my church in Los Angeles, that what women need most of all is to be relaxed and feel beautiful on the outside. They repeatedly use terms like *encouragement*, *support*, *rejuvenation*, *relaxation*, and *nurture* to describe their ministry.

In contrast to this, Scripture says our greatest need is Jesus Christ because of our sin and separation from God. Our greatest need, as women and human beings, is to know the Lord, who he is and what he wants from us. Our greatest need is not to be relaxed, because Christ calls us not to be comfortable but to comfort.

Paul the apostle writes of comfort in 2 Corinthians 1:3–5: "Blessed be the ... God of all comfort, who comforts us in all our affliction, so that we may be able to comfort those who are in any affliction, with the comfort with which we ourselves are comforted by God." In this text, he uses the term *paraklesis*, which means much more than "relaxation or repose"; it literally means "calling to one's side to give aid." In Paul's time, the word was often used as a technical term for a lawyer. The word *comfort* itself is derived from two Latin words—*cum*, which means "with," and *fortis*, which means "strength" or "brave." *Comfort* literally means "to give one strength." "Comfort," writes missionary Amy Carmichael, "is not soft, weakening commiseration; it is true, strengthening love."[4]

Jesus calls us to the hard way, a narrow way, to bear our own cross, to give away all we have. These things are not easy to hear; they never have been. "He who has ears to hear, let him hear," Jesus repeats eight times throughout the gospels. He knew his words were burrs in people's sides, splinters under their fingernails.

I will not deny that women are stressed, overworked, and sometimes aren't good at drawing healthy boundaries to ensure that they are rested and healthy, but tea parties, luncheons, crafts, and spas are secular, not scriptural, methods of achieving rest. Jesus did not say, "Come to me, all of you who are weary and burdened, and we will have a tea party." Why, then, do we hold on to these methods so tightly? Where do we draw the boundary line? At what point do we move, as my friend Tami would say, "from meaningful restoration for the purposes of spiritual formation to narcissistic navel-gazing"?

I think many of the same assumptions about women undergird women's ministries around the country, which is one reason why we are hearing so many rumbles of dissatisfaction. The assumptions do not resonate with many of us, and it seems our souls know something is not right about the way we do women's ministries. Something is deeply wrong, and it goes all the way down to our foundation—to what it is we believe about women and their needs. It is one thing to say you believe that women's greatest need is Jesus; it's another thing to work that out in ministry practice.

Some might argue that these troubling views are the inheritance of complementarianism, but I disagree, for many complementarian churches offer a rich diet of theological training and sound biblical teaching. Mary Delk, the minister to women at Bethlehem Baptist Church, is a complementarian who has built a theologically sound women's ministry around four pillars: prayer, study and application of the Word, fellowship, and serving. "But Christian fellowship," Mary says, "naturally happens when women serve together ... much more so than when you just go to the spa together."

Dr. Sue Edwards, also a complementarian, is an associate professor of Christian education at Dallas Theological Seminary. She is the mentor professor for the Women in Ministry concentration in the doctor of ministry program. Dr. Edwards has mentored several Christian female leaders who are challenging the contemporary women's ministry paradigm. "In my position at DTS," she says, "I've been able to show the faculty and students what women can bring to the table. It's absolutely imperative we have more women ministering ... my greatest blessing is watching men begin to view women differently."

These are two complementarian women who are adamantly opposed to ministry based on fluff or felt needs and are instead focused on the great service women can do in the kingdom of God. In contrast, the current women's ministry majority paradigm has lost sight of that purpose and mission by prioritizing the Western definition of comfort and convenience. Women do not need to be relaxed and pampered as much as they need to know that they have a role to play in kingdom building, something much greater than themselves.

SISTERS AS STRANGERS

Within just a few steps of crossing the border into Tijuana, Mexico, you are plunged into a completely different world. Gone are the green hills, the manicured lawns, and skyscrapers made of steel and glass. In Tijuana, the hills are brown and covered with makeshift homes. The air is crowded with the sound of car horns and the smell of car exhaust. Barefoot children peddle snacks and trinkets to visitors. An old woman, whose face bears more grooves than the number of years she has lived, crouches in the shade of a building, holding a paper cup containing the coins of passersby. She says nothing, looks out at nothing, just holds her paper cup. You are alert and prepared for the unexpected because you know you are in a different culture.

But step on a plane and fly around the world to St. Petersburg, Russia, and the differences appear to be less severe. Apart from the store that sells only vodka and the televisions blaring American television shows in Russian, everything is pretty similar. The same lines to claim baggage, the same lighted billboards you would find in any airport in the United States or Europe, people dressed in similar clothes. You relax, because it seems familiar.

Until it's not. While you are dining in a nice Italian restaurant, a cat jumps on your table and your hosts invite it to eat from their plates. Escalators steeper than black diamond ski slopes take you more than one hundred meters underground to the metro. Nobody smiles or speaks on the streets. A Russian grandmother, a *babushka*, worries about your appetite and persistently asks you to eat great quantities of food at each meal. A truck driver stabs his tires with a knife when his truck gets stuck underneath an overpass. The experience is jarring and disorienting because the chasm between your culture and theirs is greater than you expected.

Similarly, there is a chasm between the older and younger generations in the local church, and the massive depth of the division is surprising because it can seem that we are much more similar than we actually are. After all, we attend the same church, live in the same community, share similar beliefs, and for the most part, have similar day-to-day experiences. But the ways Baby Boomers (born between 1946 and 1964), Gen Xers (born between 1965 and 1977), and Millennials (born between 1978 and 2002) see, experience, and interpret the world differ greatly because the accelerated rate of cultural change has made it difficult, if not impossible, for older generations to keep pace with the younger.

Much has been written on how the cultural differences between the generations impact the local church in regard to evangelism and types of worship services, but little has been said about how these generational differences impact gender-specific ministries in the church, especially women's ministries. Besides having a flawed philosophical foundation, women's ministries are not actually working, largely because of the cultural differences between the older and younger generations. We know they are not working, because studies show that women are leaving the church. From 1991 to 2011, the number of women who attended church on a weekly basis dropped from 55 percent to 44 percent.[5] Anecdotally, many women leading traditional women's ministries have admitted to me they have had difficulty retaining younger women.

As a Millennial, when I examine the women's ministries of the local church, I get that same disorienting feeling I had in Russia when the cat jumped on our table. I am always surprised and, honestly, a bit repelled by the descriptions of the various events offered by the typical women's ministries. The women for whom they seem geared are strangers to me. I don't know anybody like that. I have experienced a lot of guilt over this, but have come to realize that my reaction is largely grounded in two aspects of my identity as a Millennial: a lack of experience with walls between genders and a desire for *communitas*.

While I do not claim to speak for an entire generation, studies show that these traits are predominant enough among Millennials that I can speak with a certain degree of confidence about why traditional women's ministries aren't working for Millennials.

LACK OF GENDER WALLS

I grew up in a town of about fifteen hundred people, and the fifty people I went to kindergarten with were the same fifty people I graduated with. Our junior year, we got a new principal I'll call Mr. Jacobs. Mr. Jacobs brought in a number of sweeping changes, including a derogatory attitude toward women. He shamed female teachers by belittling them in front of students.

A few months before the school year was up, we held our senior class elections, and during those elections, the boys decided that Mr. Jacobs was right: women weren't very smart and they couldn't be trusted with leadership roles. All the girls laughed because we thought they were joking. We had grown up with them, and they knew better. But the boys refused to vote for the girls, and since boys outnumbered girls, only one girl was elected to student council. The boys did not think boys really were smarter than girls, but they thought it was funny to emulate what we all thought—what we had all been taught—was a backward way of thinking.

Millennials were raised on the shoulders of giants who labored to make inroads for women's rights. From the cradle, we have been taught that we are the same as boys, and most of us have never imagined we are not as good as boys. We have always been able to wear pants and any color of the rainbow, not just pink. We were told we are smart and can be anything we want to be and anybody who said otherwise—even a school principal—was foolish.

We are so convinced of our equal ontological value that even when we experience gender discrimination, we don't know it. King's College professor Elisabeth Kelan notes a study that described Millennial women's experiences at work: "Although these young women confronted gender inequality, rather than focusing on gender, they were happy to accept their age and lack of experience as reasons for their experience ... these women stressed they were individuals and were not thinking in categories of men and women as structuring their experiences."[6]

All our lives, the only place most Millennials have ever been separated from males has been the restroom. Everywhere else, even at church, we have been together. For us, there were no real walls between the genders, and we are not used to highly feminized environments. In fact, many of the symbols associated with traditional women's ministries are actually a bit offensive because of how congruent they are with older stereotypes about women.

"A symbol," wrote T. A. Kenner, "is something that represents something else by association, resemblance, or convention."[7] For Baby Boomers, teas, teacups, pictures of dainty high heels, decorations, and crafts are symbols that mean "rest and respite from work and home." It is just a little something women can do when they get together. Millennials don't get the message that this is what women can do; we get the message that this is *all* women can do.

DESIRE FOR *COMMUNITAS*

In the 1985 movie *The Breakfast Club*,[8] five unlikely characters—a jock, a rebel, a nerd, a popular girl, and a social misfit—experience a deep sense of community when they realize they have more in common than they thought. Though they attend the same school, they don't know one another because their respective social roles prevent it. But Saturday morning detention, an experience that anthropologists call liminality, bolsters a sense of community by minimizing differences.

The Breakfast Club portrays the kind of organic community that Millennials long for. Every day, we interact with more people than the average person interacted with in a year just a hundred years ago. Yet in a world so connected, we are still longing for deep community because of the social isolation inherent in our virtual and suburban lifestyles. That is one reason we seek out meaningful experiences through service. It is not that we are particularly more altruistic than previous generations;[9] it is because those types of experiences bring us to a place of liminality—a space outside of our normal environments—where *communitas* happens. *Communitas* is a type of "supercommunity" that "happens in situations where individuals are driven to find each other through a common experience of ordeal, humbling, transition, and marginalization."[10]

As with happiness, you can't get authentic community by aiming for it. Real community happens not through structured programs but by focusing together on a common purpose. As the French poet Antoine de Saint-Exupery wrote, "Love does not consist in gazing at each other, but in looking outward together in the same direction."[11]

Missiologist Alan Hirsch argues that we need to change our mindset when it comes to community. Rather than approaching it with a consumer mindset, focusing on what community can do for us, we need to approach it with a missional mindset, focusing instead on "me for the community and the community for the world."[12]

This is where the concepts of liminality and *communitas* come in. When anthropologist Victor Turner studied the rituals of the Ndembu people in Zambia, he identified three phases of the rites of passage when young boys become men. Until the age of thirteen, boys are raised with women in the female quarters. One night tribesmen from the male quarters "kidnap" them and take them into the bush, where they fend for themselves for six months. If they survive, they are reintroduced to the tribe as men.

Turner called this six-month period the liminal, in-between phase. The young men were not boys, but they were not yet men. Here, in this liminal phase, the young men bonded, developing intense relational bonds that Turner described as *communitas*. As the five members of the Breakfast Club experienced, in the unstructured, transitory liminal phase, social differences (like economic rank, gender, and ethnicity) fall away and leave room for people to experience deep relationships based on equality and common experience.

Communitas develops between soldiers during war, between students away at college, between volunteers on mission trips. *Communitas* developed among the Israelites as they wandered in the desert after the exodus and among the disciples during Jesus' earthly ministry. Turner believed that liminality was a permanent condition for all Christians. "The Christian is a stranger to the world, a pilgrim, a traveler with no place to rest his head. Transition here has become a permanent condition."[13]

"*Communitas* is ... always linked with the experience of liminality," Hirsch comments. "It involves adventure and movement, and it describes that unique experience of togetherness that only really happens among a group of people inspired by a vision of a better world who actually attempt to do something about it."[14] Millennial women are thirsty for that deep sense of togetherness, for *communitas*, even if they are not quite sure how to express it. That is why many of the social events offered by traditional women's ministries have difficulty attracting and retaining younger women. It is not that we don't want community; we want real community so deeply we are unwilling to be satisfied with substitutes.

MINISTRY BY CHRISTIAN WOMEN

We need a new way to do women's ministries, a way that is grounded in the assumption that women can be trusted with ministry. We need to do away with the image of the well-coiffed, perfectly put-together Christian woman and make room for diverse ethnic groups, the single woman, the single mom, the working mom, the work-at-home mom, the theologian, the scholar, the woman nurturing a radical dream for ministry; for all these are Christian women, and all have a part to play in the building up of the kingdom of God. If so few women are able to go to seminary, the local church is the only opportunity for women to learn and grow. If we are not reaching them, equipping them, we are not fulfilling the Great Commission.

We need a little dirt under our fingernails, evidence of digging deep into our local communities to meet the needs of the economically and spiritually impoverished. We need to go back to the cradle of women's ministries, back when women's ministry was ministry by Christian women rather than ministry to Christian women. We need a women's ministry guided by the ultimate truth that "the good life" is a life in which we dare mighty things, getting to know who God really is (as opposed to our safe ideas about him), introducing him to others, and caring for the poor, the orphans, and the widows. We need ministries that teach women what it means to be brave, to sacrifice, and to take risks to oppose the great injustices of our time. There are battles to be fought today, just as much as there were in the times of the Grimke sisters and Frances Willard.

We still need to learn Scripture, but it must be balanced with mission and action in order to avoid the spiritual obesity that results from learning Scripture but never applying it. Women need classes on theology, hermeneutics, liturgy, and the classical virtues. We need coffee shop conversations and symposiums that tackle difficult questions. The commitment to missions needs to stretch beyond annual mission trips, perhaps by adopting a local, ongoing missional project like a local women's shelter. If the majority of households in your community are single women and mothers, what kind of ministry can you build to meet their needs? These are just beginning suggestions; we need more conversations about how to build effective women's ministries.

CONCLUSION

"One of our biggest external struggles as a church is something called brain drain," says Annie George, a professor in Adoor, India. "All the talented people go abroad, and what we have left in our churches are people who cannot and a few who will not go abroad." In many ways, I think we have the same problem in our churches in America. Gifted and talented women are leaving the evangelical church because there is no place for them. We do not acknowledge their giftedness and strengths, even in—especially in—the very place we would hope to find it: our women's ministry programs.

That said, change is hard, and it must be done carefully. To bring about changes in the way we do women's ministry, we must demonstrate sensitivity to the current paradigm. Perhaps the best way to build the new way is to build it first alongside the old. Current women's ministry directors and senior church leadership can select lay leaders who can build a supplemental women's ministry—a skunk works project—that operates outside the traditional women's ministry, ironing out the kinks until it is ready for an official launch. There are a plethora of ways we can change the way we do women's ministries; each church community must evaluate what will work best for their given situation.

Refocusing women's ministries from ministry to Christian women to ministry by Christian women will go a long way in helping us to equip and retain female Christian leaders who are passionate about daring mighty things for God. The next step is figuring out how to handle the challenge of limited opportunities.

CHAPTER 9

LOCKED DOORS AND DETOURS

ON LIMITED OPPORTUNITIES

There are those who say fate is something beyond our command. That destiny is not our own, but I know better. Our fate lives within us, you only have to be brave enough to see it.

—Princess Merida, *Brave*

No one would have mistaken Gladys Aylward for a leader, at least not in the beginning. She was born in London into a working-class family, received a basic education, and became a parlor maid when she was fourteen years old. People believed she was inadequate and unqualified for anything beyond the role of a parlor maid.

"I was told that I must offer myself for a certain missionary society, and eventually I went to this society's college for three months." In the end, she was rejected by the missions agency because she failed theology. "By the end of that time the committee decided my qualifications were too slight, my education too limited to warrant my acceptance . . . I left that committee room in silence, all my plans in ruins."[1]

But Gladys was determined to go to China, a place where millions had never heard the gospel. Though she carried the disappointment of the missions agency's rejection with her for the rest of her life,[2] this disappointment did not deter her from what she felt God had called her to do. She got another job as a parlor maid for a missionary couple and saved her money for four years until she had enough to buy a one-way overland ticket to Yangchen, China. During that time, she learned many lessons from her employers. "Never before had I met anyone who trusted [God] so utterly, so implicitly, and so obediently." They told her stories of their life overseas and that God could be trusted. "God never lets you down," they said to her. "Maybe He doesn't answer your prayers as you want them answered, but He *does* answer them. Remember, no is as much an answer as yes."[3]

Gladys bought that ticket to China and traveled alone in dangerous territory through Russia and China. She partnered with aging missionary Jeannie Lawson to found Inn of the Eighth Happiness, a place for travelers to rest and hear the gospel message. When the government began outlawing the practice of foot-binding,[4] she served as a foot inspector and had great success in places where there had been great resistance to foot inspectors. She quelled a riot at a men's prison that was so hostile even officials were afraid. She brought the men's grievances to the officials, which led to improved living conditions.

Gladys adopted unwanted children and cared for wounded soldiers. When the war intensified, she led one hundred children more than one hundred miles over the mountains to the safer province of Sian. For these things the people gave her the name Ah-weh-deh, "virtuous one." At the end of her life, she wrote, "My heart is full of praise that one so insignificant, uneducated, and ordinary in every way could be used to His glory for the blessing of His people in poor persecuted China."[5]

Gladys Aylward's experience of being rejected by the missions board reminds me of one of my first experiences with rejection. On top of all the awkwardness associated with being in junior high, the middle school years were a tremendously tumultuous two years for me. My mother had been sent to rehab for addiction to prescription drugs, and shortly after that, my parents divorced. I had always been a social misfit with only a few close friends, but the weight of my family's personal problems made it even harder for me to relate to others.

So one day at lunchtime, holding my tray of food, I scanned the lunchroom for a place to sit. Every table seemed so unwelcoming. Eventually, I spotted one where a couple of my friends sat. As I approached, I saw one girl (a girl who was lauded around town for her "Christian kindness and character") lean over and whisper to another girl as she saw me approach. That girl then got up and cut me off before I got to the table. "Halee," the girl said, "we talked about it, and we decided you're not good enough to sit with us."

Tears flooded my vision and my heart dropped like a rock. I said nothing and simply took my tray, loaded with food, and threw it away. I went to the bathroom and wept. How rejected and alone I felt that day. Not good enough. And it was not the last time. My life has been punctuated by similar moments of rejection. My years as the "invisible adjunct," doing the same work or more as full-time faculty without the title or the benefits. The academic dean who said I was not good enough, lacking the sufficient "breadth and depth" for a tenured faculty position simply because I had never held a tenured position before. (And how does one come to hold their first tenured job, then?)

Worthless. Insignificant. Not good enough. How abrupt those words sound. How final and absolute. How tall and wide they stretch across our way. Is there any way around them? Rejection is always painful, no matter how old you are or what context you experience it in. Our experiences of rejection have sticking power, and they stay with us all our lives, impacting our self-worth and stripping us of the confidence we need to take bold risks and dare mighty things.

As female leaders, we have to come to terms with the fact that we will probably experience rejection because of the limited opportunities for women. Unfortunately, this is the reality, and we have to be honest about it.

BARRIERS FOR FEMALE LEADERS

Even as recently as the 1970s, women experienced visible barriers to positions of influence that were described as "the brick wall." Companies that were looking for new hires would post signs that read "Women need not apply." Because of the efforts of tremendously courageous men and women who ushered in a revolution for women's rights, the late 1970s brought forth a tidal wave of changes in the way we think about female leaders, and we have not been the same since.

For a time, the challenges for women came to be described as a "glass ceiling," meaning that although it seemed that men and women had equal advantages, women could go only so far before they reached an "invisible" barrier. But even more progress has been made, because many leadership experts believe that the metaphor of the glass ceiling is outdated and needs to be replaced with the image of a labyrinth,[6] a pattern with a single winding path from the entrance to the center. Leadership experts Alice Eagly and Linda Carli write, "The obstacles that women face have become more surmountable, at least by some of the women some of the time. Paths to the top exist, and some women find them. The successful routes can be difficult to discover, however, and therefore we label these circuitous paths a labyrinth."[7] The metaphors we use to describe the primary challenges for female leaders matter because they are part of the storytelling that can compel change. If we view the challenges to women in ministry as a brick wall, we might give up. We might get angry. If we view them as a glass ceiling, we might be tempted to be satisfied with less.

But if we view them as a labyrinth, we begin to see that although the path from point A to point B is not a straight shot, it does lead to a certain destination. The goal, whatever it may be for you or for me, is not absolutely beyond our reach; all it takes is a little knowledge and skill to navigate our way to the place God is calling us to.

JUST HOW LIMITED?

In 2012, the Barna Group published a report based on a telephone survey of 603 women over the age of eighteen. In the survey, women were asked about how well their church supported them as leaders. The research aimed to figure out how women felt about their leadership opportunities at church. Here are some of the results:

- Three-quarters (73%) of all women say they are making the most of their gifts and potential.
- Three-quarters (72%) say they are doing meaningful ministry work.
- More than half (59%) claim they have substantial influence at their church.
- Slight majority (55%) expect their influence to increase.
- Eighty-four percent of women believe their churches are open or mostly open to female leaders.
- Yet 31 percent say they are resigned to low expectations.
- Twenty percent feel underutilized at church.
- Sixteen percent say their opportunities are limited by their gender.
- Thirteen percent feel underappreciated at their churches.
- Eleven percent feel they are taken for granted in their churches.

The Barna Group points out that though the numbers reflecting negative experiences are small percentages, "given that about 70 million Americans qualify as adult churched women, this amounts to millions of women in the US today who feel discouraged by their experiences in churches."[8] It is also worthwhile to consider the possibility that women who have had more negative experiences have already left the church and thus weren't part of the study. Finally, the positive responses don't automatically mean that these women have never had to deal with disappointments in church.

When I attended seminary, one of the big questions people debated was whether seminaries should accept the tuition money from female students if they knew there were limited opportunities for them once they graduated. When women eschewed tradition-ally accepted paths to ministry (such as Christian education) to study alongside men in the master's of divinity, the doctor of ministry, and the doctor of philosophy programs, how well did the seminary sup-port them? Did they affirm women's commitment to their calling?

Since 30 percent of seminary students are women, but women lead only 10 percent of all churches, it is a fair question to ask. Not that seminaries ought to deny admittance to female students, but since they know women's opportunities *are* limited, they should provide vocational support for their female graduates, assisting them in finding ministry work. But as we mentioned in chapter 3, it is impossible to estimate exactly how limited women's opportunities are when it comes to traditional ministry paths like leadership in local churches, because there is no governing organization able to keep track of what is going on in all local churches.

We can safely assume that while there are more leadership oppor-tunities for women in the local church than there have been in the past, those opportunities are still somewhat limited. We have taken a step closer to equal opportunities for women, but we are not there yet. Further, we learned in chapter 3 that more than half (59%) of all female members of the Christian Leadership Alliance hold either upper leadership positions (18%) or first-line or middle man-ager positions (41%). When compared to all women serving in CLA organizations (and not just those who are members), the percentage of female leaders is probably much lower.

So, then, we have two stories: women report that for the most part, they feel as though they are making the most of their gifts and do not feel limited by their churches, and yet the numbers tell us that opportunities for women are limited in both the local church and parachurch organizations.

This discrepancy may have several roots. First, we discussed earlier that one of the limitations of self-report is that people often give what they perceive to be "the right answer" or an answer that reflects things as they ought to be, not as they actually are. It is possible that women experience more limitations than they actually reported in the survey. Second, it may be that the women in the survey had lower aspirations for the use of their gifts, and thus are satisfied with fewer leadership opportunities. Third, it may be that churches have many leadership opportunities for women apart from the role of senior pastor or paid leadership positions.

Regardless of how the majority of women feel about their opportunities in the local church, the lack of women in higher levels of leadership in both churches and parachurch organizations means that the challenge of limited opportunities remains an important obstacle to address. And we cannot dismiss the experiences of the women who reported feeling underutilized by their churches. Because of this, it is important to discuss how to respond to the challenge of limited opportunities. Will we have the courage, despite the pain of rejection, to be faithful in our response to locked doors and detours?

THE TWO TEMPTATIONS OF THE UNDERVALUED

Sue Edwards didn't even like women when she was growing up because her difficult, dysfunctional mother had made it impossible for her to relate to women. As an adult, she dealt with severe depression until a neighbor invited her to a women's Bible study. "Those women re-mothered me," she remembers. It wasn't long after that that Sue discovered her calling to teach Christian women. "I'd been called to teach the Scriptures in-depth, so I went to DTS [Dallas Theological Seminary] to become a better Bible teacher."

After graduating, she began to attend a local Baptist church. "The very first day we joined, the senior pastor gave me permission to start a ministry to women." Sue plunged into the work, often volunteering more than sixty hours per week. Despite the great amount of work she was doing, she felt as though her efforts weren't really appreciated. "I learned a lot about ministry, and I worked long hours, but I never went to a staff meeting. I never felt like I was part of the team, and I really grieved that."

Sue's story illustrates how women can do all the right things, go above and beyond what duty requires, and still be greeted by a locked door or a dead end. When we are bone tired and weary after putting in long hours of ministry only to be met with ingratitude, resistance, or indifference, it is easy to fall into one of two temptations: the temptation to leave church altogether or the temptation to bury your gifts and just give up.

In his book *Resignation of Eve*, Jim Henderson shares the story of Susan Hall, a licensed therapist with a troubled history with the church. After college, she started a women's shelter through her local church and served there for six years, but she didn't believe she received the support she needed from her church to grapple with her tough questions. Eventually, Susan left the church. "I finally admitted I was done with the church," she confesses. "I quit going and I haven't been back since. But I didn't quit my faith—not yet. I still considered myself a Christian, even if it was the non-churchgoing type."[9]

In a study conducted in 2011, the Barna Group found that women's weekly participation at church has fallen from 55 percent to 44 percent. The majority of women no longer attend church on a regular basis. The Barna Group reports, "No population group among the sixty segments examined has gone through more spiritual changes than women. . . . The only religious behavior that increased among women in the last 20 years was becoming unchurched. That rose a startling 17 percentage points—among the largest drops in church attachment identified in the research."[10] It is easy to point the finger at people like Susan and attribute their desertion to a lack of faithfulness or commitment to the Christian faith, but I think this view greatly minimizes how painful it can be to feel invalidated or, worse still, invisible.

The second temptation for women who have experienced rejection is to take the path of least resistance and allow their dreams to be silenced. After being rejected or neglected over and over again, they take a more passive role at church and in life in general. As Simone de Beauvoir writes in *The Second Sex*, "Many of the faults for which women are reproached — mediocrity, laziness, and frivolity — simply express the fact that their horizon is closed."[11]

Julie was acquainted with rejection. She had a twelve-year-old boy named John whose father didn't hang around long enough for him to be born. Her parents begrudgingly took her in, and her mother watched John while Julie worked and took classes for her BA degree at the community college. Her hands told the story of how hard she worked; her knuckles were swollen and dry, the skin surrounding them loose and wrinkled as if they had been dunked in dishwater too often.

Julie worked in construction and was studying to be an architect. It was a "man's job," but she loved carpentry and designing spaces in which people would live and work. What made the job so hard was the fact that her male colleagues didn't respect her opinions or ideas; they'd just toss them aside like a dirty Kleenex. She kept her head down, worked hard, and tried not to let it hurt her feelings. But it always did.

John was starting to ask questions about his father, questions Julie didn't have answers for. She wondered if other single moms struggled like she did. Her church was a smaller one, mostly made up of young families, but there were a handful of other single moms in the congregation. Maybe they felt as lonely and lost as she did. The church didn't have a ministry for single parents, and Julie wondered if God was calling her to start one. The more she thought about it, the more convinced she was of his will. So after sketching out a ministry proposal and plan, she enthusiastically brought it to the senior pastor.

Pastor Bob wasn't a mean man, but he was busy and skeptical

about Julie's proposal. He wanted to focus on traditional families and he didn't feel like separating single parents from the rest of the congregation, especially given how few single parents actually attended the church. He heard Julie out, but politely declined—it just wasn't a good fit for the church at the time. Julie knew she shouldn't have taken it so personally, but she did. She was heartbroken because the rejection cut two ways—at her identity as a single parent and at her ministry plan. Her horizon, as de Beauvoir would say, was closed.

Julie continued to go to the church, but it wasn't really the same. She felt she was little more than a body warming the pew. Having mustered all the courage she had to approach Pastor Bob the first time, she felt it wasn't likely she would ever be able to do so again after that initial rejection.

When I am at church, I often think about people like Susan and Julie. I wonder how many Susans have left the church, and how poorer we are as a church because of it. I wonder how many Julies there are sitting through the service, brimming with latent potential they themselves are probably unaware of. What might happen if *all* God's women were mobilized and released to do the kind of ministry they have been called to and created for? What would happen if we unlocked the doors?

For those of you like Sue, Susan, and Julie, women who have been wounded by locked doors and detours, I would like to share three strategies I have found to be helpful when navigating these challenges.

EYES FOR OPPORTUNITY

It began, I think, when I was a little girl just trying to please Daddy, and it grew (as monsters often do) over the years, feasting on a steady diet of my insecurities and a razor-sharp awareness of my many faults. Somehow that little girl trying to please Daddy became a girl and a woman who really believed, deep down, that the whole world would fall apart if she failed, if she was not perfect in every way.

Grooves that deep are not easily smoothed, and it has taken me a long time to amend that fixed, core belief by realizing the difference between failing and being a failure. When we are confronted by locked doors and detours, it is tempting to blame ourselves, believing we got what we deserve because we are, after all, just a failure. Nothing new to see here, move along, folks. Even now, when I know better, it is my gut reaction.

I am a failure.

Let me say this to all of you who, like I did, faced the disappointments of locked doors and shouldered all the blame: you are not a failure. Yes, you may fail; if you live courageously, you *will* fail. But you are not a failure. I do not care where you heard it—your dad, your mom, a teacher, the "mean girls" at school, a boyfriend, a husband, maybe all of them. You are not a failure.

You are *not* a failure, and the second you believe it is the second your eyes will open wide to all the ministry opportunities around you. Though opportunities for women appear to be limited (for now), we can't let those limitations discourage us from seeking ways to exercise our giftedness to bless others. That's the very thing we cannot do. "As each has received a gift," Peter writes, "use it to serve one another, as good stewards of God's varied grace" (1 Peter 4:10).

If upper leadership positions aren't available to you, maybe you could lead from a second chair, like Melissa Brosch, the high school director at Calvary Church in Santa Ana. Melissa is not the senior pastor, and though she is a licensed pastor and her role is a pastoral one, she does not officially claim the title Pastor. Yet she is still able to do the actual work and ministry to which she has been called. As Melissa says, "One of the victories I'm most proud of is becoming a high school pastor. I never thought that would happen."

We can also learn from our sisters in Africa and take advantage of volunteer, lay leadership opportunities. Emily Chengo, the African director for ALARM (African Leadership and Reconciliation Ministries), says that though women aren't officially acknowledged as leaders in their churches, they nevertheless have significant influence. "We have a leadership development training institute for women (WLTI) because we know women play a major role in leadership development in churches," Emily says. "They may not be pastors, but they are leaders." This WLTI is a twin to the men's program, the Pastoral Leadership Training Institute, which is also a three-year program to train leaders, who in turn train and mentor others.

You can also volunteer (or get a job) for a Christian nonprofit organization. Katherine Holloway left a corporate job to volunteer at ALARM. From the Dallas office, she coordinates the activities of full-time staff and oversees fundraising. "Many people come to me and say, 'What can I do to help?'" Katherine says, "Even I struggle with that. Sometimes it's so overwhelming I don't know what to do. But Africa is a place where one person can make a difference. It's not me trying to change a continent; I'm empowering others to empower others."

Maybe you have a knack for writing and a nose for news, like Katelyn Beaty, managing editor at *Christianity Today*. "My calling," Katelyn said, "is to work with words, knowing that my words have the capacity to shape hearts and minds." Or maybe, like Sarah Sumner and Sue Edwards, you are called to Christian academia. People like to thumb their noses at academia as if to say it is not "real ministry," but this is a mistake, and a costly one. I believe that Christians' minimization of scholarship has truncated our ability to impact culture. Our blades are dull and no match for the thick meat of culture.

This is the first principle for dealing with limited opportunities: open your eyes to *all* the opportunities for ministry by paying attention to the needs of your community. Pray that God grants you wisdom to recognize ministry opportunities, even the most obscure.

SHE DID WHAT SHE COULD

I remember when I was about six years old riding home in the car with my mother when a song came on that has haunted me throughout my life. My mother loved the dark, grungy music of the '60s and

'70s. (Most of it I didn't like.) But one song struck me so deeply I remember the exact stretch of winding country road we were driving on when I first heard it. It was a song by a group from the 1960s called Ten Years After titled "I'd Love to Change the World."

"I'd love to change the world, but I don't know what to do," the writer laments. "So I'll leave it all up to you." I have never been able to shake those words since hearing them all those years ago. When I see the enormity of the world's pain coupled with my limitations, they come back to mind. "I'd love to change the world, but I don't know what to do."

When we face the struggle of limited opportunities, when doors close and are double-bolted from the inside, it is tempting to fall back on those words. "I'd love to change the world, but I don't know what to do." We may even go so far, at least in our actions (or inaction), to live out the next phrase: "So I'll leave it all up to you."

Elisa Morgan, President Emeritus of MOPS International, recently wrote a book titled *She Did What She Could*.[12] In this book, she takes us back to the story of the woman who anointed Jesus with perfume. This woman demonstrated love and adoration for Jesus in the face of mockery and unkindness, and was praised by Jesus, who said, "She did what she could ... what she has done will also be told, in memory of her" (Mark 14:8–9 NIV). It wasn't a huge act. She didn't draw thousands of people toward Christ. She didn't perform a miracle. She did what she could, given her limitations. Small. But what seems small to us wasn't small to God; it was a beautiful act treasured by him.

Elisa urges us to ask ourselves, "What if ... I did what I could? What if I acted with what I have? What if I acted right where I am? What if I acted because it might matter?" Mother Teresa would tell her sisters, "Don't look for the big things, just do small things with great love. The smaller the thing, the greater must be our love."[13] By living out this principle, she was always on the lookout for opportunities to love—great or small. She knew, too, the paradoxical nature of the principle: that no act of great love is small. "To the good God nothing is little because he is so great and we are so small."[14] Did any leper think her simple embrace a small thing? The thirsty, a glass of water? The hungry, a meal? None of these things are really small, for they have the power to change a life.

When we consider the future of ministry *by* women, we need to remember the woman anointing Jesus' feet with oil and Mother Teresa's principle. Let's not be discouraged by locked doors and limited opportunities and all that we cannot do. Let's do what we can, praying the Lord guards our hearts against cynicism and bitterness and self-doubt. This is the second principle for dealing with limited opportunities: do what you can. Now. Today.

BOUNCE

The story of the oak and the reed is a story with many roots. Some attribute it to early Judaism and some to Aesop. The fable tells of an oak and a cluster of reeds that grew together deep in a forest. Both experienced the same weather conditions, but each responded in different ways. During a particularly strong storm, a gale of wind blew so fiercely that the oak, firm and unyielding, snapped in half.

When it fell among the reeds, the oak said to the reeds, " 'How is it that you who are so frail and slender, have managed to weather the storm, whereas I, with all my strength, have been torn up by the roots and hurled into the water?' 'You were stubborn' came the reply, 'and fought against the storm, which proved stronger than you. But we bow and yield to every breeze, and thus the gale passed harmlessly over our heads.' "[15]

The reed illustrates the power of resiliency, an important trait in leaders, especially when it comes to locked doors and detours, when someone says no or when things don't quite work out the way we planned. Resiliency is *bounce*, the ability to spring back into original form after enduring outside pressure or force. Our success as leaders is largely dependent on how resilient we are—how quickly we can recover from setbacks or difficulties. Resiliency is a fusion of three skills: optimism, perceived competence, and perseverance.

OPTIMISM

Optimism and pessimism are ways of viewing the world. The pessimist assumes the worst while the optimist assumes the best. When she does not get the job, the pessimist says, "I don't know what I was thinking, applying for that job. I don't have what it takes. No wonder they passed me over, especially in this economy." When the optimist doesn't get the job, she says, "Wow, that's disappointing, but I can understand. I do need a little more experience before applying for a position like that. Something will work out soon; I'll find the perfect job."

The same circumstance happened to both people, but they interpreted it in radically different ways. As Romans 8:28 tells us, "We know that for those who love God all things work together for good, for those who are called according to his purpose." Not that all circumstances are good, but that all things work together for good in the end. This type of optimism is grounded in reality, not a denial of reality.

PERCEIVED COMPETENCE

Perceived competence is the confidence that you have the skills and abilities for a given situation. Perceived competence is grounded in a crystal-clear awareness of reality, your strengths, and your vision— where you need to go. Perceived competence wards off anxiety and the fear of rejection, which can cripple both our performance and our boldness in taking risks.

When vacationing in Florida with my family a few years ago, I was caught in a rip tide and pulled half a mile out in the ocean. As a former lifeguard, I knew that panicking was the worst thing I could do. Instead, I relaxed and placed confidence in my abilities as a swimmer and my knowledge of the rip tides of that particular beach. Eventually, by swimming parallel to the shoreline, I escaped from the rip tide and was able to swim to shore. As we grow as leaders, we will invariably experience situations that provoke anxiety: launching a new ministry, speaking in a new venue, taking on more responsibility. We can maintain the degree of calm necessary for navigating these new situations successfully by placing confidence in our knowledge, strengths, and abilities.

Earlier in the chapter I shared how Julie's pastor rejected her proposal for a singles' ministry. A bit more confidence in her competency to assess the need for a singles' ministry and in her ability to make the ministry successful would have helped her recover more quickly from the rejection. Rather than giving up, she would have begun to think of other ways to reach out to the singles or perhaps other ways to convince the pastor it was an important ministry for the church to offer.

PERSEVERANCE

Perseverance is the grit to keep going, to keep moving forward in the face of obstacles, disappointments, and discouragement. Aesop teaches us about the importance of perseverance in the fable "The Tortoise and the Hare." In that familiar story, the tortise and the hare are in a race, and the hare bounds ahead full steam, while the tortoise takes his time. The hare burns out and takes a nap, while the tortoise slowly plods along. Notice what the tortoise does not do. He does not say, "Well, this is a ridiculous race to begin with; I can't possibly win." He just moves forward and keeps moving.

That is the power of perseverance. Perseverance is not giving up because a certain ministry opportunity didn't work out. It means moving forward, confident that the Lord will work through your life despite limited opportunities.

All these traits—optimism, perceived competence, and perseverance—are skills that can be learned. Honing these skills will make you a more resilient leader, able to handle the setbacks that come with limited opportunities. Whatever locked doors or detours you have faced, however tempted you have been to leave the church or bury your giftedness, you mustn't edit your dreams. Do not amend them to be safer, tamer. *Dare mighty things.* As the "Last Lion," Winston Churchill, said, "Success is not final; failure is not fatal. It is the courage to continue that counts."

Some may wonder why I have not said more about fighting for more opportunities. There may be times for that, and God will help you discern what to do in a given situation. When you run up against limited opportunities in your organization, you will have to decide what God is calling you to do. Is he calling you to continue to work in that organization, or is he calling you somewhere else? Those are difficult decisions that individuals must decide given their particular ministry context. I have offered these principles, though, because I believe that ultimately they will open up more opportunities in healthy Christian communities. What happens to us is not nearly as important as how we respond to it.

CONCLUSION

Out the back door of our parsonage in Glendora, California, there is a trail that locals call "Poop Out." It is not really even a trail at all; it is a firebreak that shoots straight up and over several mountain crests, built by the Los Angeles Fire Department to train new recruits to fight mountain fires. At 11.75 miles up the trail, you are exhausted. It is hot; you are running out of water and food; and you cannot tell exactly where the top is. Does it ever end? If it is your first time up, you're tempted to quit. The path down is appealing, easy.

You don't know that at 12.25 miles, just half a mile away, the trail ends at the apex of the mountain and you will be rewarded with incredible views in every direction. To the north, the snow-capped San Gabriel Mountains are majestically clothed in low-lying clouds. To the east, an endless ridge of mountains are skirted with communities. To the south lies all of greater Los Angeles and, beyond that, the Pacific Ocean. To the west you see downtown Los Angeles, Hollywood, Malibu, and the sun glinting off the Pacific. You are amazed, awed by the view, and humbled by the realization that if you had given up at mile 11.75, you would have missed it.

For women, the path to ministry is littered with obstacles, and limited opportunities only make the trail more difficult. There are times when it is tempting to quit. But can any locked door keep God out? Can any missed ministry opportunity prevent God from working in your life? "For we are his workmanship, created in Christ Jesus for good works, which God prepared beforehand, that we should walk in them" (Eph. 2:10).

God created you; you are not an accident. He has a purpose for you; your passions, your dreams, are not arbitrary. God will not be kept out. No matter how limited our opportunities are, God can and will work through women. He always has, even in times when women were much more limited than we are now, and he always will. If we are faithful in our response to resistance and rejection, if we continue to press forward though we are tempted to retreat, we will be rewarded with the blessing of knowing we have made a difference in the lives of others.

In this chapter, we've explored how to face the challenge of limited opportunities with resiliency. Now let's talk about sex—and how it can impact the ministry potential of women.

CHAPTER 10
LET'S TALK ABOUT SEX

BUILDING HEALTHY CROSS-GENDER MINISTRY RELATIONSHIPS

Let's talk about sex for now ...
It keeps coming up anyhow
Don't decoy, avoid, or make void the topic
Cuz that ain't gonna stop it.

—Salt-N-Pepa, "Let's Talk about Sex"

Over pizza and soda at Woody's Wood-Fired Pizza in downtown Golden, Colorado, Amy and I talked about female Christian leaders. Amy was a vice president for a Christian nonprofit in Los Angeles. She had been with the company for several years; it was the first place she applied after college. She started as an administrative assistant for the president, but senior leaders quickly realized she had a knack for business and a mind for problem solving.

Amy quickly moved up through the ranks, becoming the first (and only) female vice president. The president, the board members, and the other vice presidents appreciated her ability to navigate complex organizational challenges, but there was one challenge that completely stumped her: how to get the president to meet with her one-on-one about the ins and outs of running her department. What were his goals? Where did he want the department to go? What did he think about the direction she had been taking it? She had her vision; she wanted to be sure it matched his.

"Technically, we have leadership meetings," Amy told me, "but all the decisions really get made over coffee at Panera, and since he promised his wife he'd never have coffee alone with a woman, I'm left out in the cold. I don't really know how good of a job I'm doing because he won't meet with me to give me any kind of feedback."

The president's avoidant behavior was an ongoing problem, but the breaking point came at the first leadership retreat. "It was so embarrassing. The president, the board, the other VPs and I all went to Rancho Capistrano Retreat Center for the weekend. But I was excluded from everything except for a couple of meetings. I spent most of the time in my room or wandering the grounds. Nobody talked to me or interacted with me, and I wondered why I was even there. They acted like I was dangerous."

Over the years, I have heard similar stories from many women. The female children's pastor who is overlooked by the senior pastor. The female midlevel manager at a Christian ministry who can't find a sponsor—someone to promote her and her abilities—because all the senior leaders are men unwilling to "risk" building a collegial relationship with a female leader. The new, first female employee who gets lost in the organizational culture because the men feel they have nothing to teach her—their experiences are too different, their paths too divergent. The female vice president left out of decisions because they were made in the men's room.

This is not just a Christian problem. In a recent study, Catalyst, a Manhattan-based research firm, found that "exclusion from informal networks" tied with "gender-based stereotypes" was the top barrier preventing women from further advancement. Forty-six percent of women cited this as a reason they were unable to progress in their organizations. One woman reported, "I have the old problem of all the men going to the bathroom to make a decision. And I'm going … well, I wasn't there … and then they go play golf. Again, I'm not there. You're treated differently. And it's subtle. I don't think I was always meant to be excluded, but at the time, I didn't play golf. And I wasn't about to go in the men's room!"[1] The problem of female exclusion reaches beyond the Christian faith and beyond American borders as well, surfacing in every country where women have positions of influence. Though our Christian identity adds another dimension to the difficulty in forging collegial, platonic relationships between men and women, it doesn't have to be negative. Christians can lead the way, rather than fall behind, on how men and women can relate to one another in the workplace.

The word *platonic* means "of, relating to, or being a relationship marked by the absence of romance or sex."[2] It comes from Plato, a Greek philosopher who, ironically, was thought by many to be the first feminist. Georgia Harkness notes that in Plato's ideal republic, women would have "complete sex equality, with women taking their places alongside the men not only in education, but in service in battle and in the highest offices of the Senate."[3]

Sun Tzu was a military strategist and general who penned *The Art of War*, a book that many consider to be a masterpiece on the philosophy of war and strategy. In thirteen chapters, he outlines several principles for understanding conflict. What makes the book so unique is that many of the principles can be applied to life as well as to war, teaching the reader how to handle conflict effectively. In one section, Sun Tzu offers this piece of strategic wisdom: "If you know the enemy and know yourself, you need not fear the result of a hundred battles. If you know yourself but not the enemy, for every victory gained you will also suffer defeat."[4]

In our highly sexualized culture, women are often portrayed as little more than sex objects and men as animals who can't control themselves. In contrast to this narrative, Christians can model appropriate, God-honoring cross-gender relationships in which women are treated as sisters worthy of dignity and men as respected brothers. If Christians are to learn to build effective cross-gender relationships for the purposes of ministry, we need to understand ourselves and our "enemy," which is, in this case, our historical and cultural context.

MALE AND FEMALE PLATONIC RELATIONSHIPS: A HISTORY

One summer day when we were eleven years old, my friend Katy and I were playing catch in her front yard. As we tossed the ball back and forth, we talked about the future and about what we wanted to do with our lives. I told Katy I wanted to be like Indiana Jones, an adventurous professor who traveled the world. Confusion crept over her face as I said this, and she paused, holding the ball. "A professor?" she repeated in surprise as she threw the ball. "Well, my daddy says I'm good for nothing but to be home, barefoot and pregnant." She said the words so simply, so effortlessly, yet they fell like a cinderblock between us. At first I thought she might be joking, but I could tell by her expression that she was not. Her eyes were dewy with tears. "Katy," I said, "don't you believe that for a second! Your daddy is a *hillbilly*." It was a naughty thing to say, but honestly, I have never lost sleep over saying it.

I couldn't imagine my parents saying anything like that to me. How defeated she must have felt to have a parent like that. He had tripped her at the starting line, before she ever really got to race. For me, college was not an option but a requirement. Like most Millennials raised (for the most part) outside the local church, my equal footing with men was so assumed it was never even mentioned.

What we didn't know is how new this concept of equality was—barely a generation old. Millennials are really the first generation in history for whom the equality of men and women is a given—so much a given that many of us think feminism isn't necessary anymore. Talking to us about feminism is like talking to a Southern Californian about frostbite; they have heard of it and it sounds unpleasant, but thankfully, they don't have to worry about it because it is not an issue for them. As I mentioned in chapter 8, Millennials don't notice gender discrimination even when we experience it ourselves. That is why it is so hard for us to conceptualize that for most of human history, women have been viewed as inferior to men, fit for nothing but domestic work and childbearing.

The Western concept of women's inferiority goes back to Athens in the teachings of Socrates, Plato's tutor, and Aristotle, Plato's pupil. Socrates often referred to women as "the weaker sex" and argued that "being born a woman is a divine punishment, since a woman is halfway between a man and an animal."[5] Plato, sandwiched between Socrates and Aristotle, held a more favorable view of women, but Aristotle furthered Socrates' views, believing that Plato's Republic was impractical. Classics professor Sarah Pomeroy writes, "Aristotle elucidated in detail the range of women's inferiority, from her passive role in procreativity to her limited capacity for mental activity."[6]

Greek philosophy was a tremendous force in shaping Western civilization as we know it. That means that the idea of women's inferiority is buried in the foundation of our culture. You can find the concept threaded throughout many of the writings and teachings of the early church fathers, such as Saint Clement of Alexandria, Tertullian, Saint Jerome, Saint John Chrysostom, and Saint Augustine.[7]

Though there have been illustrious queens, esteemed female saints, and periods of chivalry in which women were honored and respected, and though the *level* of inferiority may differ from culture to culture, the fact remains that throughout history, women have never been perceived as fully equal to men.

This long and storied history is one reason why it is so difficult for men and women to build platonic working relationships. Women and men have been working in the same spheres only since the early 1970s. That's just forty years. If you have a young earth creationist view and believe that humans were created around 10,000 years ago, that means men and women have been working together for .4 percent of human history, less than half a percent.

If you have a theistic evolutionary approach, and date the beginning of the human race to around 200,000 years ago, the percentage drops to .02 percent. To draw those numbers closer to home, if you are thirty years old, .4 percent of your life is 43.8 days, a little under a month and a half of your entire life; .02 percent is just over 3.65 days of all your thirty years.[8] That's how recent the changes are in the contexts and ways in which men and women relate.

HE'S JUST NOT THAT INTO YOU: PLATONIC RELATIONSHIPS AND CULTURE

I spent many summers from late elementary through junior high palling around with my friend Ben. We spent our days playing baseball, tag football, or just hanging out watching movies. We talked for hours on the phone about nothing in particular. Despite all the time we spent together, there was never a single second of romance.

Aside from Harry Potter and Hermione Granger, I have never seen a movie that accurately depicts the kind of relationship Ben and I had. In almost every movie depicting friendships between men and women, the friendship is a prelude to romantic love. If a friendship doesn't end in romantic love (as is the case in *My Best Friend's Wedding*), it is always portrayed as disappointing and less than ideal.

As a culture, we prize Eros love more than friendship love — if we even really believe that friendship love exists at all. C. S. Lewis writes, "When either Affection or Eros is one's theme, one finds a prepared audience. The importance and beauty of both have been stressed and almost exaggerated again and again ... very few modern people think Friendship a love of comparable value or even a love at all."[9]

Affection is the love of a mother or father for their child, or the child's love for their parents. Eros is romantic love. Eros can include sexual desire, but it is distinct from it. Friendship, in contrast, is the least natural of all the loves. We don't biologically need friendship in the way we need Eros and affection. "Without Eros," Lewis writes, "none of us would have been begotten and without Affection, none of us would have been reared."[10] Friendship is the most disposable of the loves.

We don't know how to do friendship in the classical way the ancients saw it, between two or more of the same gender, let alone friendship between a man and a woman. Lewis goes on to say, "To the ancients, Friendship seemed the happiest and most fully human of all loves; the crown of life and the school of virtue. The modern world, in comparison, ignores it."[11]

In addition to this relational poverty, perhaps *because* of this relational poverty, we live in the context of a highly sexualized culture in which women are objectified and men are reduced to animals. From the cable television show *Toddlers and Tiaras* to padded bras for preschoolers, the sexualization of females begins at an early age. Photographs used to depict reality — a visual snapshot of time — but now virtually all the images that come to us via magazines or television are either edited or airbrushed to eliminate features that are deemed undesirable. They depict *un*-reality. Many advertisements dismember women's bodies altogether, presenting only certain body parts to sell a product.

When a culture is sexualized, everything is sexual — even hamburgers, or at least that's what Carl's Jr. would have us think. And when everything is sexual, nothing is. The "sexual liberation" we think we have because "sex" can be had with no strings and no commitment really isn't sex at all; it's only an artificial version that can never really satisfy us in the way sex was intended to.

When people are sexualized, they begin to believe that their value is wrapped up in their physical attraction. In her book *America's Women*, Gail Collins notes that "while teenagers in 1900 made resolutions about how to become better people, a century later they almost always fixated on perfecting their bodies rather than their character."[12]

HARRY AND SALLY WERE RIGHT: SCIENCE AND PLATONIC RELATIONSHIPS

Culture also teaches us that when we see a friendship between a man and a woman, we automatically think the man always wants more; he wants the relationship to be sexual. We don't really believe men are capable of being "just friends" with a woman. In the iconic film *When Harry Met Sally*, Harry makes a pass at Sally and she declines, saying they can just be friends. Harry, though, doesn't believe that's possible.

Harry: "You realize, of course, that we could never be friends."

Sally: "Why not?"

Harry: "What I'm saying is—and this is not a come-on in any way, shape, or form—is that men and women can't be friends because the sex part always gets in the way."

Sally: "That's not true. I have a number of men friends and there is no sex involved."

Harry: "No, you don't."

Sally: "Yes, I do."

Harry: "No, you don't."

Sally: "Yes. I do."

Harry: "You only think you do."

Sally: "You say I'm having sex with these men without my knowledge?"

Harry: "No, what I'm saying is they all *want* to have sex with you."

The scene is so familiar that parts of it have become colloquial expressions. But science now seems to indicate that Harry was right. Since cross-gender friendships are a historical novelty, there is very little research on them, but recently, researchers at the University of Wisconsin—Eau Claire conducted a study to analyze attraction in cross-gender friendships. In the study, eighty-eight couples who were friends but not in a relationship completed a confidential survey regarding different aspects of their relationship. Here is what the researchers discovered:

- Young men experience more attraction to their friends than young women do.
- Men knew their friends were less attracted to them than they were to their friends, but they still overestimated how attracted their friends were to them.
- It did not matter if men were in committed relationships with other women; they still reported the same level of attraction to their friends.
- Men in committed relationships and single men both expressed a similar level of a desire to go on a romantic date with their friends.
- Women in committed relationships reported the same level of attraction to their friends as single women, but they did not want to go on a romantic date.[13]

In a second study, the researchers analyzed emerging adults and middle-aged adults to see if attraction varied over time or with changes in marital status. Here is what they found:

- Middle-aged men report much lower levels of attraction to their friends if they are in committed relationships.
- All participants—young, old, male, female—thought attraction was a cost or a complication of the friendship rather than a benefit.
- Among those who did see attraction as a benefit in the relationship, it didn't matter whether the person was in a committed relationship.[14]

Both men and women report feelings of attraction to their friends of the opposite sex, though the intensity of the attraction declined if the person was in a committed relationship. These studies support previous research that indicates one of the challenges for cross-gender relationships is addressing the issue of sexuality and attraction in that relationship.

Cross-gender collegial, working relationships are different from cross-gender friendships because working relationships tend to be compulsory while friendships are voluntary. We get to choose our friends, but we do not usually get to choose our colleagues. That said, researchers from Lancaster University found that people are likely to forge the strongest friendships of their lives with their colleagues, especially if they work in stressful environments.[15] Therefore, these studies on cross-gender friendships can help us build effective collegial relationships by raising our awareness of these realities.

A second challenge for cross-gender relationships is how to present that relationship to others. Because of our history and culture, others will always expect that more is going on than simply friendship. That's why we need not only to be *aware* of our historical and cultural context but also to *respect* it as we seek to build Christian, cross-gender relationships that honor the Lord. The fact that cross-gender relationships are a historical novelty occurring in one of the most sexualized cultures in human history explains why cross-gender relationships are so awkward—and that's before you even add in the complexities rooted in our identity as Christians!

CROSS-GENDER RELATIONSHIPS BETWEEN CHRISTIANS

So how do Christians traditionally deal with cross-gender collegial relationships, especially Christians in committed relationships? Let's look first at two of the most common ways. The first is what I call the "Bubblewrap Approach." This approach is characterized by high boundaries and little or no interaction between men and women. Billy Graham is often cited as an exemplary model of this approach.

During his active years, Graham was so committed to personal purity and a desire to maintain an image of godliness that it is said he refused to ride in an elevator with a woman or to counsel her without a third party present. It's not necessarily that he didn't trust himself; he wanted to be above reproach. It is the same approach adopted by Amy's boss, along with many others.

There are several strengths to this approach. First, it is grounded in a strong desire for personal purity. In an age when Christian leaders often fall into sexual indiscretion, destroying ministries, families, and their witness to the world, it is hard (if not impossible) to overestimate the value of personal purity for Christian leaders. Second, it decreases the number of opportunities for sinful behavior to develop. In Ephesians 4:27 terminology, it doesn't "give the devil a foothold" (NIV). Third, it is often (though not always) rooted in a desire to honor spouses and marriage vows.

Yet there are several weaknesses to this approach. First, as more and more women become leaders, this approach becomes unsustainable. Men and women have to work together and form strong cross-gender alliances with people other than their spouses. Second, female leaders are penalized because, as men usually hold higher offices of leadership, they have no mentors or sponsors to promote them in the organization. Some women don't even have the access to executive leaders they need just to run their departments well. Third, this view is often (though not always) rooted in troubling views of women, views that reduce women to sex objects. Because everything is sexualized, women are something to fear rather than honor as sisters in Christ.

The second approach is what I call the "Daredevil Approach." This approach is characterized by low or no boundaries in cross-gender relationships. There is a small but growing movement among some evangelicals on the opposite extreme of the Bubblewrap Approach. Because of grace and Christ's death on the cross, boundaries aren't necessary. Since men and women live in (theoretically) equalized environments, we need to tear down the old boundaries established between men and women because they are nothing more than corsets that force us to comply with external (and outdated) standards. Since Jesus was not afraid to enter into friendships with women, neither should we be. We ought to be free to enter into cross-gender friendships in which we can take vacations alone with one another, go out to dinner, and buy extravagant gifts for one another on holidays, Valentine's Day, and birthdays.

The strength of this approach is that it acknowledges the changes that have occurred in society regarding the equality of men and women. Second, it is an honest attempt at a more grace-based way of perceiving the opposite sex. Third, it seems—at least on the surface— to be the antidote to some of the negatives that resulted from the Bubblewrap Approach. In all likelihood, there are men and women who, exposed to the Bubblewrap Approach all their lives, deemed themselves (and their sexuality) as untrustworthy and shameful.

However, there are several weaknesses in this approach. The first and most concerning is the disregard for the historical and cultural context. Not being mindful of this is about as wise as going for a swim in the ocean without knowing the force and direction of the undertow. When a scientist named Chuck Blay studied drowning victims in Hawaii, he found that 75 percent were visitors and over 90 percent were white males in their forties and fifties.

"One of the things that kills us in the wilderness, in nature," comments survival writer Laurence Gonzales, "is that we just don't understand the forces we engage.... Even when we're told, even if we understand it at an intellectual level, most of us don't embrace the facts in that emotional way that controls behavior."[16] That's why so many visitors and white males drown in Hawaii; they don't understand the undertow and they get too comfortable with their own strength or their perception of it.

The Daredevil Approach makes a similar mistake: it relies too much upon a perception of strength to resist sexual temptation. Furthermore, the Daredevil Approach isn't sensitive to the surrounding culture. In Acts 17, the apostle Paul met the Greeks where they were, demonstrating sensitivity to their cultural narratives in order to communicate the truth of the gospel. When building cross-gender relationships, we need to forge them in a manner that is sensitive to how others will interpret them. A relationship with no boundaries—with significant periods of alone time, romantic gifts, or even physical affection—will not be interpreted well by Christians or non-Christians given our highly sexualized culture. Finally, this view minimizes personal purity and the biblical command that Christians, especially leaders, are to be above reproach (1 Tim. 3:2; 3:11; 5:22; Titus 1:6–7; 2 Peter 3:14).

Fortunately, there is a third way, a way I think incorporates the strengths of both the Bubblewrap and Daredevil approaches while at the same time avoiding their weaknesses.

THE THIRD WAY: MEN AND WOMEN AS CO-LABORERS AND ALLIES

Judith Shoemaker and Bruce Butler are co-pastors of Glendora Friends Church in Glendora, California. Unlike most co-pastors, Bruce and Judith aren't spouses. Judith started at Glendora Friends Church as a youth worker, working her way up through the ranks as the youth pastor, assistant pastor, and then as associate pastor alongside Bruce. After several years working together as senior pastor and associate pastor, Bruce and Judith realized they had accomplished the major goals they had set for the congregation, so they prayed about what came next. At the time, the church was undergoing several changes that led Bruce and Judith to believe God was calling them to be co-pastors.

When they proposed it to the congregation, the church was not ready for the idea of co-pastors, let alone a male-female co-pastor team; but they trusted Bruce and Judith, so they approved a one-year term. The elders in particular worried about the ability of a man and a woman to work together in such a close capacity. Over time, the congregation warmed to the idea, enjoying the benefits of the male-female team.

First, the vision of the church was more robust in the sense that it reflected male and female perspectives. In their role as senior pastor and associate pastor, Bruce and Judith executed Bruce's vision for the church. As co-pastors, they worked on their joint vision for the church. Second, when someone needed counseling, they would be able to meet with a senior pastor, but weren't forced to meet with someone of the opposite gender because men could be counseled by Bruce and women by Judith. Third, the congregation had the uncommon privilege of learning how women and men could work with one another, playing off each other's gifts and strengths. At the end of the year term, the congregation and leadership were so pleased with the arrangement that they approved it as an ongoing call.

Bruce and Judith demonstrate a third way men and women can approach cross-gender relationships: as co-laborers and allies. Their example provides four foundational ways we can begin to build these types of relationships in our own churches and Christian organizations.

1. Establish clear corporate thinking about men, women, sexuality, and cross-gender ministry. Evaluate what your church or organization really believes about men and women. What do you say you believe? What do your actual policies and procedures say about what you believe? Are there men and women distributed evenly across all levels of leadership? Why or why not? Are men and women encouraged to work together in teams? Is that working? Why or why not?

The Scriptures tell us that we are brothers and sisters created in the image of God. What this means is that we have to be careful in our corporate and individual thinking to view one another in this manner, rather than in the manner of our culture, which depicts women as dangerous temptresses and men as little more than animals.

When Judith was going through seminary, she had difficulty finding a mentor because there were no female leaders in her denomination and men refused to work with her. "Men would say to me, 'I can see you're gifted and I can see you're called, but I'm not going to work with you,'" Judith says. "They thought it would be too tempting and dangerous." In contrast, Bruce wasn't afraid of Judith. He recognized her as a strong female leader, pushed her to get the MDiv, and made sure she took all the right steps in the ordination process.

More men need to emulate Bruce's example and sponsor or mentor women. I am glad that so many Christian men want to honor God and their wives, but if men and women are to work together successfully, we have to find a way to address "the sex part." Men need to be willing to put aside their fears and help women in the workplace; women need to be sure they really aren't dangerous and do what they can to dress modestly and act in appropriate, God-honoring ways.

2. Establish clear, wise boundaries in advance. Any attempt we make to build platonic relationships between men and women needs to bear in mind the weight of history and our cultural context. Clear boundaries, rather than simply restricting us, provide us with safety. For example, Bruce and Judith drew up a contract with their spouses with very strict guidelines, including never riding alone in the car together, meeting together with the secretary present, and granting spouses access to emails and phones. Not only did this provide a safe place for their working relationship to grow, it gave their congregation confidence in their relationship. "Be transparent," Judith advises, "and don't kid yourself about what could—or couldn't—potentially happen."

Proponents of the Daredevil Approach point to Jesus' relationships with various women to argue against traditional boundaries. While Jesus did break down some of the social barriers between men and women, he didn't demonstrate the same level of intimacy with women as he did with his disciples. There is wisdom in discerning the difference between a colleague and a close friend of the same gender, with whom you might share more intimate details about your life.

In their book *Mixed Ministry*, authors Sue Edwards and Kelley Matthews make the excellent point that though there are some universal boundaries, some boundaries will differ from person to person or situation to situation. For example, you may find that you are more sexually attracted to one colleague over another. Sexual attraction is normal and it happens to everyone! Fortunately, there are ways we can deal with it without resorting to either extreme of segregating ourselves or giving in to temptation.

Edwards suggests evaluating each circumstance and color-coding the attraction level. When she found herself deeply attracted to a man she worked with, she had a "red-alert battle plan" ready. She delegated projects in which he was directly involved and minimized contact. She was prepared to leave altogether.[17] It is important to evaluate each situation and do what you can to stay out of "the red zone."

3. Ensure that you are spiritually healthy and remain connected to the Lord. Stay close to the Lord through the Word and through prayer. Practice the disciplines. As we will see in the next chapter, our spiritual health impacts every aspect of our calling and role as leaders, but especially so when it comes to building and maintaining godly relationships, because our relationship to God orients and prioritizes all our other relationships.

4. Implement strategic organizational policies that bolster women's development as leaders. Finally, larger organizations can implement certain policies to ensure women are not penalized due to issues related to gender. First, create a mentoring culture by establishing a formal mentoring program. Design a system to pair senior members with junior members, a formal professional development plan to set goals for the mentoring relationship, and a method to monitor the program.

Second, recognize the value of sponsorship programs and encourage male and female sponsors to take on female protégés. Research indicates that both mentors and sponsors are critical to the development of a leader. Mentors are senior colleagues who provide advice and feedback, while sponsors are advocates promoting you and your skills within the organization.[18]

Third, find ways to integrate women into informal networks. Evaluate where the bulk of the decisions are made within the organization — are they at lunch, over coffee, at the golf course? Find ways to include female leaders. This helps to forge relational bonds needed in the workplace and ensures that female leaders are present when important business decisions are made.

CONCLUSION

The strategies outlined in this chapter may seem a bit artificial at first, but it's like when you decide to practice a new spiritual discipline. It feels awkward at first, forced, because it is, because you are not yet the kind of person you want to be; through the work of the Holy Spirit, the discipline helps make you into the type of person who "prays without ceasing" or quotes Scripture by heart. We aren't yet the people we want to be — men and women who can work easily together without "the sex part" getting in the way. We might as well be honest about that. These strategies help us to be honest about who we are and who God calls us to be and help us to focus on our ministry task rather than on each other.

As Father Cantalamessa writes of two lifelong, cross-gender friends, "There was certainly a very strong human bond, but it was paternal or fraternal in kind, not spousal … they really didn't spend their whole lives gazing at each other and feeling good together."[19] They were in love not with each other but with God. In the film *Francis and Clare*, Francis walks through a field and Clare follows behind him, playfully putting her feet in his footprints. "Are you following in my footsteps?" he asks her. "No," she replies, "much deeper ones."

CHAPTER 11

THE AUDACITY OF COURAGE

MOVING FORWARD through FEAR

Fall seven times; stand up eight.

—Japanese proverb

In his record-breaking, international bestseller, *Quo Vadis*, for which he won the fifth Nobel Prize in Literature, Henryk Sien-kiewicz relates a story from the apocryphal book the Acts of Peter. In the story, upon hearing the words of the Lord and a message on chastity from Peter, the concubines of Agrippa I flee his house in order to remain pure. Perplexed and grieved because he loves them,

Agrippa begins to seek them, and when he finds that they are with Peter, he becomes angry and seeks to put Peter to death.

When fellow Christians hear of this plan, they urge Peter to flee Rome. At first, Peter resists, but eventually he listens to their counsel and flees with a boy companion named Nazarius. Along the Appian Way, one of the most strategically important roads in ancient Rome, Peter sees a figure bright as the sun approaching them, but Nazarius sees nothing. As the figure moves closer, the pilgrim's staff falls from Peter's hands and he cries out, "Oh, Christ! Oh, Christ!" Peter falls to the ground as if he were kissing someone's feet. Sienkiewicz writes, "The silence continued long; then were heard the words of the aged man, broken by sobs—'Quo Vadis, Domine?' [Where are you going, Lord?] Nazarius did not hear the answer, but to Peter's ears came a sad and sweet voice, which said, 'If thou desert my people, I am going to Rome to be crucified a second time.' The apostle lay on the ground ... but he rose at last. The boy, seeing this, repeated as an echo, 'Quo Vadis, Domine?' 'To Rome' said the Apostle in a low voice. And he returned."[1] In that profound, life-altering moment, Peter the Timid becomes Peter the Courageous.

While we have no way of knowing whether the story is historically accurate, we know Peter. How *like* Peter this was. Peter the fisherman who knew what all the learned scribes and Pharisees did not, that this Jesus was the Christ, the Promised One of Israel (Matt. 16:16). Peter the Passionate, who says, "Lord, not my feet only but also my hands and my head!" (John 13:9), and, "Even if I have to die with You, I will not deny You" (Matt. 26:35 NASB). Peter the Afraid, who denies the Lord not once but three times. Peter, the one so often swayed by emotion, yet whom the Lord named "rock." Here, in this apocryphal story, we see Peter live into that which the Lord had always called him: the rock.

The apostle Peter was a human being not so very unlike us. That was the kind of person the Lord chose. "Jesus called and transformed ordinary people—who sometimes failed him,"[2] comments Craig Keener. Through the life of Peter, we see how our internal struggles with fear, doubt, bitterness, discouragement, or even depression can hinder our service to God. The truth of the matter is that when all is said and done, the greatest challenge to becoming a successful leader isn't any external limitation; it is us. It is *our* weaknesses, *our* limitations, *our* flaws and foibles, that are the very hardest to overcome. It is not so much the enemy out there; it is the enemy in here, weakening our leadership.

WHAT IS COURAGE?

Courage is often reduced to bravery, something that is useful on the battleground, but not necessarily useful in leadership. Yet prior to 1980, Webster's dictionary defined *courage* as "the heart, the seat of one's emotions and thoughts." In the Scriptures, to "take heart" or to "be courageous" was to set one's will in accordance with the will of God, no matter what the outside circumstances, no matter how deep the chasm.

In Roman Catholicism, courage is understood to be so pivotal to the Christian life that it is considered one of the four cardinal virtues and the virtue upon which all the other virtues are dependent. "Courage," writes C. S. Lewis, "is not simply one of the virtues, but the form of every virtue at its testing point, which means at the point of highest reality."[3] What he means is this: without courage, it is impossible to exercise any of the virtues at the moment it really, truly counts. Real love, the kind of love demanded of us, is risky. Real love demands we love the enemy, love the unlovable. We are called to love the murderer, love the unfaithful spouse, love the gossiper, and love our persecutor. And when people inevitably let us down? We are to keep on loving. Love like that is risky. And risk demands courage.

In this way, courage is the soil from which all the other virtues spring. For philosophers such as Plato, Socrates, and Thomas Aquinas, "courage is strength of mind, capable of conquering whatever threatens the attainment of the highest good."[4] Courage works alongside wisdom because wisdom teaches us what ought to be dreaded and what ought to be dared. Without wisdom, courage can become recklessness (too much daring) or timidity (not daring enough). Aristotle thought courage was the perfect balance between the two.

In the healthy mind and soul, there are sound, understandable reasons for many of the internal struggles that leaders face, because they arise from real threats to our personal safety or well-being. Peter was afraid to acknowledge his relationship to Jesus for a reason: it was risky to his survival. He knew it would cost him his life to admit their relationship, as it ultimately did. That's why courage is so audacious — because it enables us to move forward toward the good we ought to do despite the strong opposition posed by our internal struggles.

In the next chapter, we will be looking at ongoing spiritual growth for leaders through the development of the classical virtues, but in this chapter, we are going to explore how exercising moral courage can help us overcome three key internal struggles for women, including fear, bitterness, and burnout.[5]

FEAR

Just as he met Peter fleeing Rome, so too did Christ meet me on the road, in the hollow days of my addiction when I was fleeing him. Christ called me to come out of that life for years before I consented. I refused to come out not because I loved the carousing lifestyle but because, like Peter, I was afraid. I was afraid to live sober because life had hurt so badly. Except for a few shining moments — eating a grilled cheese sandwich Nanny made for me on a summer afternoon; sitting behind Papa in the green John Deere tractor, reading a book while he plowed cotton — I had never really felt *safe* in all my life.

The floors of our house were made of eggshells. I never knew when the next fight was going to break out or what event would trigger the slamming doors and yelling voices. I would stay up late at night, blanket pulled up to my chin, door open, just to hear my dad laugh at Johnny Carson. I tried to give my life stability by trying to be perfect; if I were perfect, then everything would be okay. Trouble is I was not perfect. I took responsibility for things, probably because doing so gave me a feeling of control in an otherwise unpredictable environment. I kept the house clean and helped care for my little brother.

We were a dysfunctional family before dysfunctional families became mainstream, at least in our area of the world. But as was the case for most latchkey kids of the 1980s and early 1990s, for me the most painful aspect of growing up was the pervasive feeling of loneliness and fear.

I was afraid because the world didn't seem to be safe and there was this vacant place in my chest, a vacancy I didn't fully understand until I had daughters of my own. Having Ellie and Viv in my life has taught me that the vacancy I had always felt was rooted in my desire for a mommy. A mommy who chased away the monsters—both real and imagined—and created a safe place in which I could grow. A mommy who would scoop me up in her strong arms and say, "I'm so happy to be your mommy."

As it was, though, there was no safe place in the world for me, except a place in the darkness I had made for myself, and I clung to it. But God would not let me hide in that darkness. He haunted me and made it impossible for me to ignore his call on my life. One morning, right after I had moved away for college, I opened my Bible and read in Deuteronomy 30:15–18, "See, I have set before you today life and good, death and evil. If you obey the commandments of the LORD your God that I command you today, by loving the LORD your God, by walking in his ways, and by keeping his commandments and his statutes and his rules, then you shall live and multiply, and the LORD your God will bless you in the land that you are entering to take possession of it. But if your heart turns away, and you will not hear, but are drawn away to worship other gods and serve them, I declare to you today, that you shall surely perish."

In this verse, Moses appeals to the exiles, to "the next generation," to return to God in full obedience. He shows them the two
ways the Lord has set before them, and it is the very same choice
God sets before us all: life and blessings, death and destruction. If we
give up our way of living—a way of living that isn't really life at all,
but a dying way—if we give that up, we get *real life.*

But I was afraid to choose life because life is painful. It knocks
you around until you have bruises from the top of your head to the
soles of your feet, and it is not too long before you expect disaster
waiting around every corner. It is so much easier to hide, to withdraw into your shell and protect yourself. That is why choosing life,
choosing the good, demands courage: because it is risky. It is painful. You are going to get hurt. Through these words of Moses, God
was essentially asking me, "Are you going to show up for your own
life? You can turn this around. It is not too late. Come back to me.
Choose the good." And so, little by little, I did. I gave him my hollow
days and he, in turn, gave me days of texture and depth, filled with
purpose and meaning, a life oriented away from myself and toward
him and my neighbor.

Of course, choosing the good does not end the moment we
become Christian; we have to continue to face our fears or anxieties
in order to choose the good all throughout our lives. Fear and anxiety[6] can be a personal challenge throughout the leadership journey,
not just at the beginning. Leadership is risky business, and so leaders
(the good ones, anyway) will face several crossroads at which they
can either choose to give in to their fears or choose to act courageously and do what God has called them to do.

Who can count the ways there are for leaders to be afraid? We fear
taking too big of a risk, because we fear failure. We fear what other
people think. We fear we are not good enough. We fear making a
mistake. We fear being wrong. We fear rejection. We fear moving out
of our comfort zone. We fear disappointing people. We fear losing our
power or influence. We fear vulnerability.

As hard as it appears to move forward through our fears to choose the good, as difficult as our minds and our habits make it out to be, it isn't impossible. In Deuteronomy 30:11–14, we read, "For this commandment that I command you today is not too hard for you, neither is it far off. It is not in heaven, that you should say, 'Who will ascend to heaven for us and bring it to us, that we may hear it and do it?' Neither is it beyond the sea, that you should say, 'Who will go over the sea for us and bring it to us, that we may hear it and do it?' But the word is very near you. It is in your mouth and in your heart, so that you can do it."

The nearness of the Word, the do-ability of God's Word, is important, because it allays any anxieties we might have about our ability to be obedient. Whenever I say, "No, Lord, this is too difficult for me. I can't possibly do what you ask," God answers, "No, it is not too hard for you."

Through the power of the Holy Spirit, God gives us the courage we need to choose him, to choose the good through our obedience to his will. Nothing can happen to us outside of or apart from the will of God. But fear and anxiety aren't the only things in leadership that require courage to face; sometimes, it's bitterness.

BITTERNESS

In the book of Ruth, we encounter the story of Naomi. Often when we read or study the book of Ruth, Ruth's courage and conviction become the focus of our study. In the shadow of Ruth's courage and undivided loyalty, Naomi can easily be overlooked. The book of Ruth takes place in the period of the judges — a particularly dark chapter in the history of Israel, a time between the leadership of Moses and Joshua and the leadership of the kings of Israel. It was a period of foreign oppression and general anarchy, a time in which "everyone did what was right in his own eyes" (Judg. 17:6; 21:25). Naomi's troubles began when she was driven from her home because of a famine. It was a time of poor economic conditions, similar to what we know today as an economic recession or a depression.

In agricultural societies, everything depended on rain, and when no rain came, famine ensued and hard times followed. To escape the famine, Elimelech and Naomi traveled from Bethlehem to "sojourn" in Moab (Ruth 1:1). It was a temporary move that turned into ten years. Imagine for a second being driven from your home, from people and places you love, from the place you knew and where you knew your place in it. Imagine then going to a country completely foreign, built on different belief structures that are a complete contrast, even an abomination, to yours.

But even this change did not discourage Naomi. When she eventually returns to Bethlehem, she laments, "I went away full, and the LORD has brought me back empty" (Ruth 1:21). She went away full. Meaning that even in the face of her difficult financial situation, even in the midst of the loss of her home, her extended family, and people she loved, she still described herself and her life as full, probably because of her family.

And at first, the move-to-Moab plan seemed successful. They were able to find food and both of her sons were able to find wives. But then devastation came again, and Naomi lost her husband and both of her sons. Sit with her a minute. Imagine what it would be like to lose your husband, your children, or other family and friends that you rely on. Like vapors, they're there one day, gone the next.

All of a sudden, Naomi is plunged into a world of complete loss. She faced the emotional devastation of losing not only her husband and sons but also the complete security of her whole life. Her identity was gone. Her future and even her continued existence were big question marks. In this time of loss, her perspective shifted. She lost hope. She tried to send her daughters-in-law away, saying to them, "It is more bitter for me than for you" (1:13 NIV). She asked that people no longer call her Naomi, which means "pleasant or sweet," and instead call her Mara, which means "bitter." Both the circumstances of her life and her response to them were bitter.

Bitterness is a festering anger, disappointment, or resentment about certain circumstances, usually arising out of a sense that one has been treated unfairly. Researchers Michael Linden and Andreas Maercker describe bitterness as "the product of a personal story of perceived injustice ... the emotional quality is characterized by resignation (hopelessness) and anger ... this state is attributed to others (persons, circumstances) and not due to own failure."[7] The bitter person says, "My hopes and goals are lost because of you and there's nothing I can do about it."

In the Scriptures, bitterness is often associated with poison (Deut. 29:18; 32:32; Jer. 9:15; 23:15). Bitterness not only affects our spiritual and mental well-being, but, like poison, it also affects our physical well-being. Harboring bitterness can affect metabolism, immune response, and organ function, and can lead to illness. Both research and Scripture reveal that bitterness has a communicable quality to it because, like disease, it can spread from person to person.[8] Perhaps Naomi was aware of the contagious quality of bitterness when she tried to send Ruth and Orpah away (Ruth 1:8–13).

In leadership, bitterness can occur when things do not work out as we planned. Perhaps we did not get the promotion we wanted. Perhaps our efforts have not been acknowledged. Perhaps people have tried to take advantage of us (and perhaps we have let them— over and over). Perhaps our opinions, perspectives, or expertise have been overlooked. Perhaps a conflict was not resolved well.

Bitterness is particularly a danger for those leaders who answer to another: the youth pastor to the senior pastor, the CEO to the board, the vice president to the president. Like Naomi, perhaps we perceive even God acting in enmity toward us. That is the ultimate danger of bitterness: misconstruing our situation or circumstances in such a way that is not consistent with the character of God.

Since events that trigger bitterness (like Naomi's loss of her entire family) target our hopes or our goals, bitterness is rooted *in a failure to keep hoping*. Bitterness leads to discouragement, and discouragement to despair. But courage demands we keep hoping even when, especially when, all hope seems lost.

Naomi thought God had abandoned her, but he had not. As we

know, she had at her side a daughter-in-law of incredible faith and courage, and through their circumstances, God brought about a plan that ultimately ushered in the crowning act in all of creation, the salvation of people through Jesus Christ. Could Naomi, in the land of Moab, the land of great loss, have imagined this? Could she have imagined that all her pain from her bitter circumstances would bring about such blessing?

When I look at Naomi and then at my own life, I have to ask myself how many times I have let bitterness and discouragement regarding my circumstances keep me from doing what God has called me to do. How many times have I misunderstood my circumstances, not understanding or trusting that it was all part of a far greater good? Courage enables us to move through bitterness to act on the confidence that things are more than they appear to be.

BURNOUT

One of my first jobs was frying chicken at Jr.'s Food Mart, a convenience store in downtown Quitman, Texas. Since the work involved cleaning trucker toilets and serving up edible atrocities—which led me, eventually, to a lifelong vegetarian diet—I didn't like the work, but I loved *working*. This love of working has often caused me to overwork, as it did during my PhD program. While I was a full-time PhD student, commuting three times a week across Los Angeles, I also worked as an adjunct professor and a reference librarian at Azusa Pacific University. On the side, I ran an editing and writing business. All told, I put in sixty to ninety hours of work each week, every week.

I loved learning and I loved my work at APU. I enjoyed meeting with students, getting to know them and walking with them as they sought to discover God's calling on their lives. But as the years passed, my energy began to flag and my enthusiasm began to wane. A mentor tried to warn me to slow down, but fueled by anxiety about my advancing maternal age, I blew on past the warning signals. I thought energy was like the sunrise—new every morning.

Then the economic collapse of 2008 happened. For our entire marriage, Paul had been able to work out of our home, so though his company was based in Laguna Beach, we were able to live in Glendora near APU. But when the company restructured because of the economy, Paul was asked to work from the office. I had finished the coursework for my PhD, and our daughter Ellie had joined our family. Since Laguna Beach was too expensive and commuting would add another two hours to the workday, we decided to take the money we had saved over the years and move to Denver where Paul could set up a practice as a therapist and I could write my dissertation, all while being home with Ellie.

In Denver, things technically seemed to go well, but cracks started to show. We lived paycheck-to-paycheck. I missed things. I missed our dog, Laska, who had been shot and killed while staying with my parents when we moved from California. I missed waking up to the children's choir on Sunday mornings. I missed my friends, the people who really knew me and loved me anyway. I missed the little deli downtown that made the best veggie sandwiches in the world. I missed my students. I missed teaching. (Who was I now?) I missed stepping out my back door to climb a mountain without worrying about babies or snow. I missed California because in a very real sense, I was born there. Paul proposed to me there, we got married there, I finally grew into my own skin there, I became a mother there. It was home.

I worried about things. I worried about how we would pay the rent from month to month, let alone tuition. I worried I didn't have what it took to finish the dissertation. I worried about what kind of life I was building for Ellie. I worried that she would feel as insecure and unstable as I had all those years ago. For her first birthday, I had the best baker in Denver make her a custom cake, as if that might allay my fears, but she never got a chance to eat it. The night before her first birthday, she was admitted to Denver Children's Hospital with a life-threatening case of respiratory syncytial virus (RSV).

Because of our crash-and-burn insurance policy, that visit drained our savings and left us in debt.

We decided then to move to Michigan, a place neither of us had ever been, but where Paul had a standing job offer. Once in Michigan, I continued working hard on my dissertation, finishing it in three semesters rather than the usual five. In early November of 2010, I defended my dissertation, and two weeks later, I discovered I was pregnant. At the end of November, the clouds came to West Michigan. From there, everything began to unravel.

From the outside looking in, everything ought to have been all right. Paul had a secure job, I was finished with my PhD, we had a beautiful daughter with another one on the way. It started with panic attacks at night followed by a general listlessness and despondency during the day. Many of the traits I considered basic to my personality—like enthusiasm, optimism, and ambition—were gone. The fire in my belly—the one that spurred me up both figurative and literal mountains—was gone. I couldn't imagine how things were going to be okay.

I had no motivation, no hope, and couldn't imagine when life would be good again. Every day while Ellie napped, I sat in the rocking chair looking at the gray sky, trying to fight the anxiety and depression rising within me. It was an empty feeling very close to death. This burnout was so severe that it had become depression.

Burnout happens when you don't take your limitations seriously. Since leaders typically tend to be high achievers, they are at a greater risk for burnout. In his book *Margin: Restoring Emotional, Physical, Financial, and Time Reserves to Overloaded Lives*, Dr. Richard Swenson describes burnout as "severe negative margin for an extended period of time."[9] To discover how much (or how little) margin you have in your life, subtract your current load (internal factors such as personal expectations or emotional disabilities and external factors like work, relational problems, and other responsibilities) from the amount of power (skills, time, gifts, emotional and physical strength) you have.

Evaluate the energy you expend managing your load compared

to how much energy you actually have to spend. If your power exceeds your load, then you probably have sufficient margin in your life. If your load exceeds your power, you are on the road to burnout. Swenson describes burnout as a "pervasive disturbance" in the psychological, physical, and behavioral spheres of your life. People suffering from burnout can experience depression, anxiety, insomnia, fatigue, increased temper, and irritation.

Preventing or curing burnout requires courage for several reasons. First, it requires you to come to terms with your own limitations, something that is particularly difficult for women to do. Women often feel as though their shoulders ought to be strong enough to carry the weight of the world. We feel as though we need to hold everything together for everyone else. To admit your limitations is to admit that you cannot do everything or be everything.

Second, taking the steps to prevent burnout takes courage because, like salmon swimming upstream, we have to fight against the current of our society. Society tells us we need to do more, more, and more. To live a slower, more deliberate life in the context of a twenty-four-hour culture is tremendously difficult.

Third, preventing burnout requires courage because it means coming to terms with your fear of becoming irrelevant or replaceable. Sometimes we work harder and put in far too many hours simply because we want to prove our value to the church or organization we work for. We overcompensate because we do not want to become expendable. As one female leader confessed, "I ultimately had to leave my job because as a married woman, I couldn't work the same hours as my single colleagues. I was already working crazy-long hours, but my boss wanted even more. I worked too hard for too long because I was afraid my boss would think I was replaceable."

To prevent burnout, begin with a crystal-clear idea of your vision and mission. Vision is your dream, an idea of the future. What is your passion? What do you want to accomplish in one, five, or ten years? Mission is your strategy for achieving your vision. What steps do you need to take to make the vision a reality? Once you have a clear idea of your mission and vision, evaluate your load according to the four Ds of time management: drop, delegate, delay, and do. In light of your vision and mission, what activities or responsibilities can you drop? What in your schedule seems extraneous to your goals? Second, what can you delegate? Delegation is not a desertion of leadership; it is an exercise of effective leadership, an exercise we see illustrated in Exodus 18 when Moses delegated the task of judging to others. Third, what can you delay? What is less urgent than the other things on your to-do list? Schedule a time in the future to get it done, and alleviate your mind of the stress. Finally, what needs to be done? What best advances your goals?

Internal struggles will arise throughout the leadership journey. In addition to the three core issues of fear, bitterness, and burnout, we will face depression that comes with certain life circumstances: the death of a family member or even the death of a marriage. We will face anxiety with new challenges. We will face discouragement when we fail. Life can be so hard. It requires so much of us, especially those of us who are called to be leaders. That's one reason why the warrior motif has attracted me so strongly—because so much of life seems like war. I have often felt as though I had to fight for every inch of victory, for every bit of spiritual and emotional health.

This is the great challenge of leadership: to finish well by remaining a person of integrity who knows herself and knows how to conquer her demons. Courage helps us do that by propelling us forward through some of the most difficult internal struggles that leaders face, struggles that can potentially handicap our leadership ability.

CONCLUSION

As Peter the Rock advanced toward Rome, he began to rejoice and praise the Lord, knowing that he was going to Rome to be crucified. He told his fellow Christians what was about to happen to him, and urged them to remember him and not to be bitter toward Agrippa. When he approached the cross, he said, "O name of the cross, thou hidden mystery! O grace ineffable that is pronounced in the name of the cross! I will declare thee, what thou art: I will not keep silence of the mystery of the cross which of old was shut and hidden from my soul. Let not the cross be unto you which hope in Christ, this which appeareth: for it is another thing, different from that which appeareth, even this passion which is according to that of Christ."[10] What Peter learned as he willingly approached the cross is that it was something different from what he had always expected. Before, he had always perceived it as it appears to human eyes, as an instrument of torture, but now he was able to see it through the eyes of faith, as an instrument of God's grace. Peter urged his fellow believers not to depend on their senses. "Blind these eyes of yours," Peter instructed, "close these ears of yours, put away your doings that are seen; and ye shall perceive that which concerneth Christ, and the whole mystery of your salvation."[11]

With that, Peter went willingly to his death, asking his executioners to hang him upside down because he felt unworthy to die in the same manner as Jesus. As this story in the Acts of Peter testifies, courage is a way of seeing, a way of perceiving that things are not what they seem from our finite, human perspective. Courage sees that the life beyond our fears is a life worth fighting for. Courage sees beyond our bitter circumstances to the blessing God is building.

In the next chapter, we will look at the final challenge for female leaders: maintaining our spiritual growth throughout the leadership journey.

CHAPTER 12

LIVE WELL, LOVE WELL, LEAD WELL

BECOMING *a* LEADER *of* VIRTUE

In our world everybody thinks of changing humanity, but no one thinks of changing himself.

—Leo Tolstoy, *Pamphlets*

I met Jesus about the same time I met Rapunzel, Little Red Riding Hood, Madeline, and Peter Rabbit. Every night after my mother had tucked me into bed, she would read me story after story — almost as many as I asked for. At the end of story time, she would tell me about Jesus in the most basic way she could. She told me that he would be a friend to me, that I could talk to him whenever I wanted and he would hear me. She told me he would keep me company when I was lonely, give me courage when I was afraid, that he would walk beside me throughout each day. She told me that when I was ready, I could make him "King of my heart and Lord of my life."

One of my earliest memories is the night I told her I was ready for Jesus to be "King of my heart." At five years old, I knew the difference between right and wrong, and I also knew I failed to do what was right most of the time. I couldn't help myself; it felt so *satisfying* to smack my little brother when he pulled my hair. Well, to be honest, most of the time he didn't pull my hair; *I just smacked him because I could.* I understood, even on a rudimentary level, what Jesus had done for me, that he had basically managed to escape childhood without smacking his siblings or anything else. I understood he had lived a perfect life and died for me because I lived imperfectly, and I understood that asking him to be "King of my heart" was another way of asking him to teach me to live the way he did.

I threw myself into my new faith with verve, absorbing all I could about Jesus through Sunday school and children's story time with the pastor right before the "big people's church." Big church itself? With the hard-backed pews, organ music, and hellfire-and-brimstone sermons common to Southern Baptist churches of that time, not so much. I mostly endured big church. By the time I was six, Nanny says I was already preaching sermons on rejoicing in God even in hard times and turning the other cheek. But mostly, I just really loved Jesus.

"I don't think I'll say I want to be like Jesus anymore," I told my mother one afternoon.

"Why not?"

"Because he's so good and I'm so bad, it just seems … insulting to him to say it."

"Well, what would you think if someone said they wanted to be like you? Would that make you happy?"

"Yeah."

"Then don't you think it makes Jesus happy, even if you don't always do it right?"

"Yeah ... I guess so."

So I kept trying to be like Jesus. One morning during recess, a troubled little girl named Marie slapped my cheek and ran away. I chased after her yelling, "No, no, Marie! You have to slap the other cheek too!" I am nothing if not melodramatic.

But as I got older, I started noticing some things that troubled me. There were a few sex scandals that rocked the church, something I understood even then, if only in the abstract. Some of the people who attended church most faithfully, many of them leaders, were the meanest, most unkind people once they walked out the church doors. It was like they just showed up to church to save face. When my parents started having marriage problems, they didn't excommunicate us, but they ostracized us. We couldn't enter the chapel without the odious eyes of judgment falling on us from every corner.

At least it felt that way. I was confused. I was devastated. These people who said they knew Jesus were so unlike who I knew him to be, and they didn't seem sorry about it. I wasn't altogether like him either, but I tried to be, and when I wasn't, I was really sorry. We started going to church less and less, and by the time I was eleven, I was officially unchurched. Everything started to unravel from there, and when I got to college, I found a "faith" I thought much more honest: atheism.

Looking back, I can see now that had I been more mature, I could have been more gracious in the way I interpreted people's actions. Some of those people were not Christians at all, and their actions had nothing to do with Jesus or the Christian faith. Others just got so bogged down by life's disappointments and heartaches that they lost sight of Jesus and the Way. If I had been farther along in my spiritual growth, I would have been able to understand that. But there's the catch-22: real, substantial growth in Christ is impossible without community, but how can one continue in a community she does not trust?

I share this part of my story not to impugn or indict other Christians

but to show what it looks like, what it feels like, from the outside looking in. I share it to show how much is at stake when we consider the
integrity of Christian leaders. Human hearts, even the hearts of the
very littlest ones, are at stake. Human hearts weighed down by grief,
sin, abuse, hopelessness, and an untold number of other horrors. I
often wonder how many there are out there like me, who found Jesus
but then lost him because of the unkindness, the un-Christian behavior of those who said they knew him. As Christian singer Grover Levy
sings, "If you want to lead me to Jesus, you better find a better way,
'cause your life is speaking so loud I can't even hear a word you say."[1]

It's easy to blame the accusation of hypocrisy on the pervasive
spiritual blindness of unbelievers, on a failure to understand what
Christianity is all about; but in this case, I think unbelievers have
better theology than many Christians.

After World War II, the church went along with the culture and
prioritized personality over character in our leaders. We reduced
objective virtues to subjective values and equipped seminarians with
head knowledge but not heart knowledge. It was more important for
seminarians to know the business of building churches, rather than
how to build personal or communal character; more important to
know theological doctrine and biblical interpretation than to know
how that theology worked itself out in everyday life.

Even today, there aren't appropriate checks in seminaries
to ensure students have superior moral character. Seminaries are supposed to develop leaders who can lead the church with both intelligence and integrity, but there are no safeguards to ensure any level
of integrity or sound moral character. A moral monster can graduate
seminary as easily as a moral saint. What else could we call the per-
petrators of the sexual crimes committed against children in both
the evangelical and Catholic church?

Recently, a colleague told me about a situation that occurred at
the seminary where she taught. One of her students, a senior pastor
of a growing, seeker-friendly church, plagiarized a whole paper from
an article he found on the internet. When she gave him the required

zero for the assignment and confronted him about it, rather than repenting and apologizing, he attacked her through email, criticizing her intelligence, her abilities as a professor, and even her gender. He was a "paying consumer" and "was not satisfied with the product." He thought, she supposed, that his tuition money bought him an A; all he needed to do was copy his assignments.

When he plagiarized two more times a few weeks later, in compliance with school policy, she gave him a zero for the course. She did further digging and found that all of his assignments had been plagiarized, even an interview he supposedly had done with a mentor. She told him of the policy, and again, rather than apologize, he denied it, sent her more threatening, abusive emails, and took the matter to the Appeals Committee. While the committee did in fact uphold the professor's decision, no action was taken in regard to the moral character of this student, neither in regard to the cheating nor in regard to how he conducted himself toward a professor. He was encouraged not to cheat again but also assured that "it was nothing personal."

As Christian organizations, we must not value tuition money (or donations, for that matter) above the moral character of our students. The students who graduate from our programs go on to serve in Christian churches or parachurch organizations and from there have tremendous influence over the lives of many people. We must take Christian character seriously. As female leaders, we need to ensure the vitality of our own spiritual lives, not only to prevent burnout but also to be transformed "from one degree of glory to another" (2 Cor. 3:18).

THE AUTHENTIC LEADER AND A CULTURE OF CANDOR

When Stephen Covey examined leadership literature for his doctorate program, he found a curious thing: after World War II, people started caring less about character and more about personality. According to Covey, a character ethic "taught that there are basic principles of effective living, and that people can only experience true success and enduring happiness as they learn and integrate these principles into their basic character," while for the personality ethic, success was "a function of personality, of public image, of attitudes and behaviors, skills and techniques, that lubricate the processes of human interaction."[2]

For millennia, people believed that moral excellence through the acquisition of the four classical cardinal virtues (prudence, justice, fortitude/courage, and temperance) was required for successful leadership. Even today, though many deny the existence or validity of objective virtues, they still expect them of their leaders. As we discussed earlier, we are looking for authentic, transparent leaders.

In his book *The Virtuous Leader*, Alexandre Havard writes, "Heads of state and schoolteachers, captains of industry and housewives, military chiefs of staff and health care workers—all exercise leadership. People expect them to do the right thing, to be men and women of character and virtue, to be motivated by a magnanimous vision for all those in their charge. And great is the disappointment when they fail."[3] The church, for better or worse, is a microcosm of America's shifting leadership preferences. While there are still personality-driven pastors in some pockets of the United States, for the most part we have started to look for authentic leadership that is more like stewardship or servanthood, grounded in a virtuous character. We are looking for leaders who say what they mean and mean what they say, who listen to differing views, make decisions based on their core beliefs, and act in ways consistent with what they say they believe.

Most of all, perhaps, we are looking for leaders who have the chutzpah to admit their failures, mistakes, and questions. We are looking not for perfect leaders but for leaders who really want to be *good* through and through, and who, like King David, are willing to publicly demonstrate real repentance when they fail. Maybe we want authentic leaders who can admit that the Christian life isn't always contemporary-Christian-music-cookie-cutter-perfect, that sometimes it's a little more like My Chemical Romance's "Welcome to the Black Parade," fraught with brokenness and weakness.

The trouble for female Christian leaders, though, is that it can be difficult to be "authentic" by admitting one's weaknesses and at the same time maintain a certain level of authority. The road for female Christian leaders hasn't been easy, and many have gotten to places of influence because of their ability to "have it all together"—or at least appear to. For female leaders to maintain authenticity and have room to grow in the virtues, we need to cultivate a culture of candor, what leadership authors Warren Bennis, Daniel Goleman, James O'Toole, and Patricia Ward Biederman describe as "the free flow of information within an organization and between organizations and its many shareholders, including the public."[4]

To create a culture of candor, though, to be honest about who we are, churches and parachurch organizations need to ensure that leaders already have a high degree of integrity,[5] deal openly with the moral failures of leaders rather than sweeping them under the rug, and articulate and openly embrace a robust theology of repentance. As Aleksandr Solzhenitsyn writes, "In keeping silent about evil, in burying it so deep within us that no sign of it appears on the surface, we are *implanting* it, and it will rise up a thousand fold in the future. When we neither punish nor reproach evildoers, we are not simply protecting their trivial old age, we are thereby ripping the foundations of justice from beneath new generations."[6] A culture of candor demands we be people of the Word and honest about moral failure.

As for female leaders, we need to commit to continual spiritual growth through the cultivation of the virtues by practicing spiritual disciplines. This is the hardest part of leadership, for the hardest person to lead is oneself. We need to *be* the kind of people we ourselves would want to follow. To lead well, we must live well and love well.

THE VIRTUOUS LEADER

When we ditched the emphasis on character, we not only lost sound, principled leadership; we threw away our compass for finding real, authentic happiness. The ancients thought that the happy life, a life of human flourishing, was found in a life centered on an idea or a person beyond the self, "a life well-lived, a life of virtue and character, a life that manifests wisdom, kindness, and goodness."[7] In this way, the cultivation of virtues not only increases our effectiveness as leaders; it leads to a happier lifestyle.

The four cardinal virtues (prudence, temperance, justice, courage) identified by Greek philosophers and adopted by the writers of the Old and New Testaments were thought to be the virtues that all other virtues hinged upon. The apostle Paul added three theological virtues: faith, hope, and love, and identified love as the greatest virtue (1 Cor. 13:13). The cardinal virtues can be acquired and strengthened through spiritual disciplines, while the three theological virtues are gifts of the Holy Spirit. In the next section, we'll explore which spiritual disciplines can help us develop the cardinal virtues. First, let's look at how each of these virtues can strengthen our leadership.

FAITH

In twenty-first-century Western culture, we tend to think of faith as a private, personal matter, but faith is actually much more. The catechism of the Roman Catholic Church defines faith as "the theological virtue by which we believe in God and believe all that he has said and revealed to us ... by faith a man freely commits his entire self to God."[8] There are three aspects to the way faith impacts our leadership. First, faith is the grounding of the leader's personal relationship with God. In this way, faith is the filter through which we see the world, the world's needs, our calling, and the people we lead (and are called to serve). Using faith as a lens in leadership is particularly helpful for leaders when they have to make hard decisions. This aspect is important to Nikki Brown, who leads programs to cure, prevent, and raise awareness about leprosy. Nikki says that one of the most important things for a leader to have is "faith that the Lord is in control and he directs our steps."

Faith is also a confidence in God's sovereignty and providence. Tami Heim, CEO of Christian Leadership Alliance, says, "I've always been the one people rely on to deliver the bad news. People will say, 'Will you make that tough call, that tough announcement?' My strength in this area comes from a deep-seated belief that I'm doing the right thing. If there are people involved, it sits under God's sovereignty."

Faith helps leaders persevere in their calling when the call becomes difficult. Katy Wing Sundararajan sensed God calling her to a youth ministry internship in Seattle, Washington, even though she did not feel a specific call to youth ministry. "I moved out to Seattle from northern Michigan.... I did not know a single soul out there [and] I was carless. It was so hard! I was incredibly lonely, and in a brand-new setting, in a new/different ministry than I had ever led in before. Plus, the lack of a car complicated every part of my ministry involvement."

In the midst of great difficulty, Katy's faith in God's call helped her to persevere with her internship. "God did use me for good, and he taught me many, many things about myself and my gifts in ministry. God used me in relationship with junior high students, drawing them in to Jesus through my love for them and my sharing of the good news. I know God used me also through preaching and in training and helping other interns. And God blessed *me* so richly in my sense of ministerial calling and identity."

HOPE

Hope keeps us from despair, and for this reason, leaders must have a tremendous capacity for hope. "Hope is the theological virtue by which we desire the kingdom of heaven and eternal life as our happiness, placing our trust in Christ's promises and relying not on our own strength, but on the help of the grace of the Holy Spirit."[9]

Leaders see reality for what it is, and still choose to believe in God's promises. So many sorrows and disappointments in the world overwhelm even the most faithful. When we meet with tragedy, such as the death of a child or a spouse, when we get the news of cancer invading our body or the body of one we love, when we lose our job or our home, despair calls out to us because despair is easy.

One would think that hope is easy and despair is hard, but that's not the case. Despair is easy because it believes only what it sees. Hope, real hope, is grounded in a full awareness of reality. It understands the weight of death and illness and loss, but instead of buckling under that weight, it is buoyed up, believing that more than what the eye can see is at work. Leaders must lead people in difficult times and difficult circumstances.

Leaders must keep despair at bay not only in their own lives but also in the lives of those they lead. To do this, they must be willing to walk alongside their followers in the difficult journeys they face. Just as Christ is *Immanuel*, "God with us," so leaders must also *be with* those they lead through the darkest nights. In his book *Moral Wisdom: Lessons and Texts from the Catholic Tradition*, James Keenan tells the story of Pope John XXIII, who visited the prisoners of the Roman prison Regina Coeli after his first papal Christmas mass. As he stretched his hands to grasp the prisoners' through the bars of their cells, he said to them, "You could not come to see me, so I come to see you."

Keenan notes, "By that simple 'being with,' leaders nourish their community with a sense of value and self-worth often missing in human experience. As a result, leaders help make the journey more hope-filled because some of the arduousness has been alleviated."[10]

The virtue of hope helps Kim in her role as a Christian professor. Hope helps her to see the potential in others. She avoids conversations in which her colleagues put students down, and she lets them know she does not approve of such conversations. Kim comments, "Each and every person we come into contact with is a creation of God whom he absolutely adores." One semester, a particularly problematic student signed up for one of her courses. "He was a toot evidently before he came to my class. Although I knew others did not want him in their classes, I firmly believe everyone should have the opportunity to further their education." To her surprise, the student worked hard in her class and recently graduated. Having hope "in these types of situations means having God's eyes to see the potential [and] not dwelling on others' perceptions or past failures."

LOVE

While faith and hope are both necessary virtues for this life, they will pass away in the next, for our faith will be confirmed and our hopes realized. But love is a virtue for both this life and the next. Love or "charity is the theological virtue by which we love God above all things for his own sake, and our neighbor as ourselves for the love of God."[11] Throughout the Scriptures, we see the primacy of love above all other virtues. It is the gift to be valued above all other gifts (1 Cor. 13:1–3) and the virtue to be placed above both faith and hope (13:13).

There are three reasons why love is a core virtue for Christian leaders. First, love motivates us to accomplish God's purposes for ourselves and for others. Second, love rightly orients us. We are to seek leadership not for power or personal gain but because of our love for others and the commitment to ensure their well-being. Finally, love enables us to see people the way the Lord sees them and gives us the capability to love them as we love ourselves (Mark 12:31).

Love has helped Elisa Morgan motivate people to do their best. "Early on in ministry I remember a nervous bubbling in my inter-action with a certain staff member. She was a fuddy-duddy in her ideas, old-fashioned in her implementation, and seemed threatened by my youth and energy." Instead of reaching out to her with open arms, Elisa felt herself withdraw from the woman.

"Eventually, I learned that if I loved her wholly and well, in truth and honesty as well as in authentic gratitude, I could motivate her to offer her best." Elisa believes that leaders can sometimes have a wrong idea about love. "In leadership we're tempted to view love as mushy, emotional, even co-dependent. Such a faulty view of a vital leader-ship ingredient is a mistake. Love is a powerful force for any leader to master and apply."

PRUDENCE

Prudence is "the intellectual virtue consisting of the right disposition to reason about what human beings should and should not do."[12]

Prudence is the capacity to make the right decisions. In order to lead effectively, leaders must be able to exercise sound judgment by making the right decisions. Saint Thomas Aquinas identified three acts of reason: deliberating well, judging rightly, and commanding what one should do or should not do. "Commanding what one should or should not do, since it is closer to the end of practical reason (i.e. proper human action), is the chief act of prudence."[13]

In his book *The Virtuous Leader*, Alexandre Havard shows how leaders can cultivate the virtue of prudence through Aquinas's five-step process. Deliberating well requires leaders to

1. gather information and analyze it critically, discerning fact from fiction;
2. avoid rationalizations, twisting data to make it fit preconceived ideas;
3. recognize and put aside their own prejudices;
4. keep in mind the nature of their organization and their organization's mission;
5. try to foresee as many consequences of their decision as possible.

To judge rightly, analyze the pros and cons. Finally, prudence is "not only insight and foresight ... it is also command ... it directs the implementation of decisions expeditiously and with authority."[14]

Prudence has helped Gail Dudley navigate ministerial relationships with discernment. "As a woman, wife, and mother in a leadership role within our church plant, serving as an ordained pastor, I have to constantly hold things close to my chest.... Very early in ministry I experienced a devastating encounter after developing what I believed to be a true friendship. Although I had an older female mentor full of wisdom caution me about having friends in our congregation, I did not exercise discretion."

Gail realized that, though having relationships was critical to her success as a leader, she needed prudence to help her discern which relationships to nurture and set the boundaries for those relationships. "It is not that I do not extend love, because I do; but I have come to the realization that one must have boundaries while still in community.... Through the years I have grown to walk with confidence in God and to extend love, but exercise prudence as a woman in leadership."

JUSTICE

Justice is "the moral virtue consisting of the right characteristic disposition of the will to render to others what one owes them."[15] It means giving to others what they are due at all times. When we consider the term *justice*, we usually tend to think of it in two senses: the criminal justice system and social justice. Yet the virtue of justice is actually much broader, governing all relationships with others.

Plato thought that justice was the "overarching virtue of individuals (and of societies), meaning that almost every issue he (or we) would regard as ethical comes in under the notion of justice."[16]

When the virtue of justice is carefully cultivated in the life of the leader, the leader strives for the common good (as opposed to their own good), faithfully fulfilling their obligations to their employer and those they lead. They treat others with dignity and respect in all circumstances.

As leaders, there are many times when we must teach others about justice and give them courage to act justly. When Heather, a pastor in Southern California, counsels victims of abuse, she encourages them to turn in their abusers so justice can be served and so others will not be hurt. "I feel really strongly about that," Heather says. "I'm in a situation currently where I will probably be going to court with a young girl whose father abused her. Unfortunately there is a lot of injustice here on earth. But knowing that God is the perfect Judge and that someday every injustice will have to bow to Jesus is very comforting."

TEMPERANCE

Temperance is about self-control, a mastery of the mind and heart by the will. The catechism of the Roman Catholic Church defines temperance as "the moral virtue consisting of the right characteristic disposition to restrain irrational sense appetites for the greatest sense pleasures; namely, food, alcoholic drinks, and sex."[17] But temperance is really a control over excess of any kind, and in this way is connected to modesty and humility (which counteracts overinflated views of oneself and one's accomplishments).

Temperance requires that we acknowledge the good in our various passions. Havard poignantly notes, "The human body is as much God's creation as the human soul, and the passions a valid expression of human nature."[18] In this way, temperance is not about repression of those desires but is about the direction of those desires toward that which is in alignment with God's purposes for those desires. This delicate dance between the extremes of repression and indulgence is what makes self-leadership so difficult, but if leaders are to lead others, they must be capable of leading themselves.

Kristen learned to exercise temperance in regard to how many hours she put into ministry. "Before my husband and I had kids, my addiction to working was a huge issue. In ministry, need is constant, and you get to the place where you think you're the only one that can meet that need. It got pretty ugly—I actually went to therapy and got some healing. I almost annihilated my life through ministry." Since then, Kristen has learned to exercise temperance in her work schedule. "I learned people don't need me every second of the day. After I had my son, I disappeared and everything was fine. It was painful and awesome at the same time."

COURAGE

As we noted in the last chapter, courage is a principal virtue because without it, all the other virtues are impossible to exercise when they matter the most. Courage is "the moral virtue consisting of the right characteristic disposition to withstand and resist fear of the greatest difficulties, namely, mortal dangers, that hinder the will from acting in accord with right reason."[19] Courage is not the absence of fear but the willingness to move forward despite fear.

Courage enables us to keep faith when doubts swirl around our minds like flies hovering over a summer picnic. Courage enables us to keep hope when we walk through painful seasons, either our own or those of the people we lead. Courage helps us love even though love often hurts. Courage enables us to exercise prudence when the decision we make counteracts our self-interest and preconceived ideas. Courage enables us to give others their due even when it costs us time or emotional energy. Courage enables us to withstand temptations that emerge out of the good, basic, God-given desires.

Thomas Aquinas also noted another aspect of courage, one that is important for leaders: magnanimity. *Magnanimity* loosely means "greatness of soul." It is the ability to desire great things for ourselves and for others. Havard argues that magnanimity "is under severe strain these days. Modern society's weird mélange of individualism and collectivism has spawned generations of small, self-centered people on the make."[20] The heart of magnanimity is service—service to one's faith, one's country, an idea, something far beyond oneself. Magnanimity touches almost every aspect of leadership. Havard writes, "Leaders are magnanimous in their dreams, visions, and sense of mission; in their capacity for hope, confidence, and daring; in their enthusiasm for the effort required to bring their work to a successful conclusion; in their propensity for using means proportionate to their goals; in their capacity to challenge themselves and those around them."[21]

Magnanimity moved Julie Pierce forward to complete a whirlwind tour of the work Christians are doing on behalf of those trapped in slavery in Southeast Asia. She wanted to back out. "I almost left my travel buddies standing at the terminal gate. I was gripped with fear. What if something happened to my family while I was gone? What if I wasn't tough enough to tell the stories of those I would meet? What if I came back wrecked beyond repair in light of the realities I had only read about?" In the end, Julie's husband expressed the gentle reminders of the stories that needed to be told and how the team needed her.

I believe a sincere, revived interest in the classical virtues is spreading among believers and nonbelievers alike. These seven virtues are each important in the leadership process. A leader doesn't have to have each of them perfectly developed in order to lead. All that's needed is an understanding of the virtues and a willingness to grow in each of them. Practicing these virtues not only increases the effectiveness of your leadership but also leads to an increased sense of well-being and an authentically happier life.

DISCIPLINES FOR SPIRITUAL GROWTH

How can one grow in the virtues? The first three virtues—faith, hope, and love—are supernatural gifts distributed by the Holy Spirit. The final four are character traits that can be cultivated through specific habits or disciplines. Thankfully, there are many resources available to help us engage in the spiritual disciplines, but here are four areas of discipline that are especially helpful for leaders.[22]

HEARING GOD'S WORD

Hearing God's Word is important for leaders to discern God's ways, his character, and his purposes for human life. We can "hear" his Word through Bible study, devotional reading, meditation, and memorization. You don't have to stick to a rigid time to read God's Word or feel as though you have to do it every day, but it is helpful to set aside regular times to study his Word.

Before I had kids, I would often devote the first part of the day to reading and studying God's Word, but since I have had two non-sleeping children who wake throughout the night and then at five in the morning, the morning devotional time is impossible for me to keep. So even though I don't think it is ideal for me, I have found that reading Scripture at night before I go to bed is a workable solution. Other times during the day may work for you—listening to Scripture while working out, reading or meditating during lunch. Above all, it is important to find a time that works for your lifestyle.

PRAYER

Prayer is an important discipline for leaders because it teaches us to rely on the Lord, not ourselves, and keeps us centered on his purpose. There are many ways to pray; we can pray through the Scripture or even practice praying the hours. Praying the hours means praying regularly, at set times (such as morning, noon, evening, and before bed) each day. I have found that praying the hours keeps me focused on God throughout the day. It actually helps me to pray even more throughout the day.

One of the critical prayers for the Christian leader is the prayer of examen, of self-examination. Adele Calhoun writes that the prayer of examen is rooted in the desire "to notice both God and my God-given desires throughout the day."[23] Through the prayer of examen, we can evaluate our growth or struggles in regard to the virtues. What did we do well? What needs to be improved?

SOLITUDE

Solitude is a critical leadership discipline because we have to discern God's voice (and our own) amid all the competing voices we hear on a daily basis. In Luke 5:16 we read, "Jesus often withdrew to lonely places and prayed" (NIV). Solitude was a habit for Jesus.

I have found solitude to be enormously important in my own life. Not just the physical withdrawing from others but also withdrawing from social media and the internet. Both social media and the internet in general provide an enormous amount of information to process and filter. They create a cacophony of voices in your head competing for equal attention. Leadership requires a pulling away into deep solitude to pray, to listen to God's voice, and to discern our own voice and opinion on various matters.

COMMUNITY

Finally, community is an important discipline for leaders — as important as solitude. Community provides a support system for a healthy life and leadership practice. Through community, we can build spiritual friendships for companionship, spiritual direction for guidance in discerning God's purposes and presence in the leadership process, and spiritual mentoring through which a seasoned leader mentors a younger leader through the leadership journey.

Western culture undermines community because we value individualism, autonomy, and independence. None of these are bad in and of themselves, but sometimes we emphasize them at the expense of community. That is why it is important for leaders to be strategic in developing a supportive community around them.

My daughter Vivienne, just eighteen months old, is already fiercely independent. She prefers to do things on her own, and she has very little awareness of just how small she is. She refuses to let me carry her down the stairs, preferring instead to tackle the great steps with her own tiny little legs. She consents to let me hold her hand, trusting that I am a reliable guide, that my footing is sure. Just this morning as we descended the concrete steps outside our building, I slipped on a patch of invisible black ice and fell down every single step—all the way down to the sidewalk. Everything was a mangled mess: my coffee and water spilled all over the pavement, my purse dumped of its contents, and Viv, screaming in pain from landing on her arm. When I fell, I took her down with me.

Christian leadership is like that. The "young" ones, the ones with unsteady legs and unsure footing, depend on us as leaders to be reliable guides. We hold their hands and walk with them until they are steady enough to carry on without us. And when we fall, they fall with us. A virtuous character gives us sure footing from which to lead, and it inoculates us against both seen and unseen dangers.

I was not an atheist long before I realized that it took as much faith, if not a great deal more, to be an atheist as it did to be a Christian. I was not ready to believe in the God of the Bible, so I settled on the vague, twilight faith of agnosticism. Until I met Jody, a hostess at the local Applebee's where I worked as a waitress during my final years of my undergraduate degree. Jody radiated a warmth you could see in the dark. Her joy was infectious. I was curious about what gave her so much joy, so one afternoon, I asked her, "Why are you so ... happy? Joyful, even?" The moment the question escaped my lips, I wanted to reel it back. I knew what she would say: Jesus. I recognized him in her character.

Jody held my hand when I wasn't strong enough to walk the walk on my own, when the steps back to the Christian faith were too great for me. She was a reliable guide, and her footing was sure. That's God's great purpose for his leaders: to be people of the Word, people of integrity, who can serve as reliable guides to the lost and the young because they are grounded with a solid, virtuous character.

CONCLUSION

A virtuous character provides a firm foundation from which we can dare mighty things. And what is a "mighty thing"? Mother Teresa is said to have lived by the maxim, "Not all of us can do great things. But we can do small things with great love." Both Mother Teresa's wisdom and her compassion are perfectly encapsulated in that phrase. But this is what I would ask: Is it a small thing to touch a leper? To embrace one who has never been embraced? What would the leprous person say?

Is it a small thing to provide a hot meal to a dumpster diver? To give single mothers the tools they need to live successful, healthy lives? To help raise awareness about human trafficking? To pastor people through the awkward high school or college years? What about a whole congregation for twenty years? Is it a small thing to provide curriculum and training for pastors in the inner city, who deal with the biggest problems confronting humanity but for whom seminary is out of reach? Is it a small thing to teach seminary and pastor a church in India, a culture hostile to the gospel?

What about teaching Thai children about Jesus Christ from the time they are very young, before they get a chance to be trafficked? Is it a small thing to train, equip, and provide food and shelter for undocumented persons in Phoenix, Arizona, ground zero in the

illegal immigration debate? Is it a small thing to lead a congregation
in worship each and every Sunday morning even when your own
throat is choked up with sorrow? Is it a small thing to train church
and community leaders in Uganda, Sudan, South Sudan, Rwanda,
Burundi, and Congo? To provide microloans to women so they can
build their own businesses?

Yes, in a sense, these are "small things," because anyone with the
gifts, time, and passion to do any of these things can accomplish the
goals for each of these ministry tasks. And yet if you have ever been
on the receiving end of any act of mercy such as these, you know
that these are no small things. The magnitude of an act is determined not simply by the effort put into it but also by the impact of
that act upon the lives of others. These are mighty things, and they
have the capability to inspire even more mighty things, like ripples
fanning out from the splash of a single rock in a still pond.

The future of ministry *by* Christian women is in our hands.
Despite the limitations that we come up against in our churches, in
our ministries, and in the balance of work and life, more opportunities exist for women now than have existed in the past. There is
room and reason to be optimistic about the future of ministry by
Christian women. God is calling women to share in the work of his
kingdom. And there is work to be done. We do not have to look
farther than the daily news to see how much the world needs the
compassionate action of God's people. In fact, we do not have to
look farther than our own neighborhoods or our own church communities. It is not too hard to make a difference. You can change the
world, little by little, and you can start today.

Look at your neighborhood, your church, and the town you live
in. What needs leap out at you? Are there places for single mothers to get basic items like food and clothing for little to no cost?
What do your local grocers and bakers do with day-old bread or
almost-expired food? Is there a way to get those items into the hands
of the needy, eliminating waste by feeding the hungry? Is there a
local women's shelter for women and children to find an oasis away

from abusive situations? What kind of Bible studies does your church provide?

How has God called and equipped you to meet those needs? Take an inventory of your natural and spiritual gifts and evaluate how they fit into the needs of your community. Maybe you are a natural at organizing, counseling, or teaching. Maybe you know how to motivate or encourage people in difficult times. What can you do in your context, despite the challenges you face, to act boldly now?

CONCLUSION

Act Boldly Now

How wonderful it is that nobody need wait a single moment before starting to improve the world.

—Attributed to Anne Frank

Viv, Ellie, and I are driving along the shore of Lake Michigan in the early afternoon. We are singing along to their "kids' songs" CD, a collection of old gospel spirituals sung by children. Viv and Ellie sing loud, "Wade in the water, / wade in the water, children, / wade in the water, / God's gonna trouble the water." When the song is over, Ellie asks me, "Mommy, what does it mean to 'wade in the water'?"

I tell her, "Once upon a time, God's people were held captive by people who made them do chores for nothing—no allowance and no treats. They worked very hard. But God wanted them to be free, so he prepared a home for them. To get home, though, they had to cross over a sea, like Lake Michigan right there, and cross over a river, too, like the one we cross when we go to Texas to visit Papa and Nana. Since they didn't have boats, they had to cross on foot."

"But how do they cross without boats?"

"When they walked up to the edge of the water, God 'troubled the water,' meaning he made it part right down the middle where they were supposed to cross. So the water built on the sides, and they passed over on dry land. When they got to the other side of the river, they were able to go home. This song reminds us of that story, and how God helps us when things get too hard for us."

Ellie smiles and leans back in her car seat, content with my rudimentary answer. It is all I will tell them, for now. But what I want to tell them both, what I will one day tell them, is this: God is an unchanging God. He is more certain than the sun, because with him, "there is no variation or shadow due to change" (James 1:17). He does not get tired; he is everlasting; "he does not faint or grow weary" (Isa. 40:28). This same God, this unchangeable, untiring God, the very same God who parted the waters of the Red Sea and the Jordan River, he still troubles the waters. All you have to do is be brave, be courageous, and wade out into those waters. He will do the rest.

Because people will come and put barriers that seem as great as the Jordan River in your path. Someone will want you to mute your voice or change your tune or hide your light, but you should never do that. You just be faithful to Jesus. I want you to keep on speaking and keep on singing no matter who wants to quiet you. You just wade into the water. At the end of the day, you will not be answering to those people about how you used the giftedness and *all that light* that God has blessed you with. You answer to God for that. And we answer to those we might have blessed had we the courage to carry on. Just be faithful to Jesus and wade out into the water. You are stronger than you know.

That is what I will tell my daughters. And that, in a nutshell, is what I would say to you. This is what Christian women need to know: God still troubles the waters. All these barriers we have talked about can seem so big, so frightening, so impassable—especially the challenge of the limited opportunities. As in every leader's life, many frightening things will come; some are so frightening you may be tempted not to go on. But you should. None of those things are so mighty as our God. And because he is mighty, we can wade out in the water with confidence. We can dare mighty things.

Do not settle for a safe life, with mediocre dreams that are not worthy of Jesus Christ. Commit to do something that terrifies you. Get uncomfortable. Push yourself out of your comfort zone by setting a big goal and planning the small steps you need to take to achieve it. Be courageous. Get risky. Your life matters, and you have a part to play in the future of ministry *by* Christian women. All you need is the will and the courage to dare mighty things, and this you can do with great confidence because God is mighty and this mighty God still troubles the waters. Do not wait a single moment. Act boldly now.

NOTES

INTRODUCTION

1. Matthew 19:16–26.

2. J. R. R. Tolkien, *The Return of the King*, reprint (New York: Houghton Mifflin, 1994), 155.

3. David McCullough, *Mornings on Horseback: The Story of an Extraordinary Family, a Vanished Way of Life, and the Unique Child Who Became Theodore Roosevelt* (New York: Simon and Schuster, 1981), 36.

4. Ibid., 112.

5. In his book *The Jungle* (1906), American novelist and journalist Upton Sinclair exposed the harsh, hopeless lives of poor immigrant workers in Chicago at the turn of the twentieth century.

6. Theodore Roosevelt, "The Strenuous Life," April 10, 1899, *http://www.bartleby.com/58/1.html.*

7. Todd B. Kashdan and Robert Biswas-Diener, "What Happy People Do Differently," *Psychology Today*, July 2, 2013, *http://www.psychologytoday.com/articles/201306/what-happy-people-do-differently* (accessed July 7, 2013).

CHAPTER 1: TERRA INCOGNITA

1. In this book, I have changed the names of women identified by only their first names.

2. Ruth A. Tucker and Walter L. Liefeld, *Daughters of the Church* (Grand Rapids, MI: Zondervan, 1987), 13.

3. Ibid.

4. Aulus Cornelius Celsus, *De Medicina II*, trans. W. G. Spencer, Loeb Classical Library (Cambridge: Harvard Univ. Press, 1989), 1–4.

5. John Piper and Wayne Grudem, eds., *Recovering Biblical Manhood and Womanhood: A Response to Evangelical Feminism* (Wheaton, IL: Crossway, 2006), 37–39.

6. Ibid., 34.

7. Robert Saucy and Judith TenElshof, eds., *Women and Men in Ministry: A Complementary Perspective* (Chicago: Moody, 2001), 14–32.

8. Rebecca Groothuis, *Good News for Women: A Biblical Picture of Gender Equality* (Grand Rapids, MI: Baker, 1997), 20.

9. Mary Stewart Van Leewen, *Gender and Grace: Love, Work, and Parenting in a Changing World* (Downers Grove, IL: InterVarsity, 1990), 47.

10. Ibid., 49.

11. Henri Blocher, "Women, Ministry, and the Gospel," in *Women, Ministry, and the Gospel: Exploring New Paradigms*, ed. Mark Husbands and Timothy Larsen (Downers Grove, IL: InterVarsity, 2007), 262.

12. Ibid., 277.

13. James Strong, *The New Strong's Exhaustive Concordance of the Bible* (Nashville: Thomas Nelson, 2010), *http://www.biblestudytools.com/concordances/strongs-exhaustive-concordance/* (accessed January 3, 2013).

14. Gilbert Bilezikian, *Community 101: Reclaiming the Local Church as a Community of Oneness* (Grand Rapids, MI: Zondervan, 1997), 37.

15. Ibid.

16. Carolyn Custis James, *Half the Church: Recapturing God's Global Vision for Women* (Grand Rapids, MI: Zondervan, 2011), 19.

17. Miroslav Volf, *Work in the Spirit: Toward a Theology of Work* (Eugene, OR: Wipf and Stock, 2001), 114.

18. Piper and Grudem, *Recovering Biblical Manhood and Womanhood,* 362.

CHAPTER 2: WHAT IS LEADERSHIP?

1. Eleanor Doan, *431 Quotes from the Notes of Henrietta Mears* (Glendale, CA: Regal, 1970), 38.

2. Marcus Brotherton, *Teacher: The Henrietta Mears Story* (Ventura, CA: Regal, 2006), 9.

3. Kevin Kruse, "100 Best Quotes on Leadership," *Forbes,* October 16, 2012, *http://www.forbes.com/sites/kevinkruse/2012/10/16/quotes-on-leadership/.*

4. Marilyn Chandler McEntyre, *Caring for Words in a Culture of Lies* (Grand Rapids, MI: Eerdmans, 2009), 11.

5. Warren Bennis, *On Becoming a Leader* (Philadelphia, PA: Basic Books, 2009), xxx.

6. R. M. Stogdill, *Handbook of Leadership: A Survey of Theory and Research* (New York: Free Press, 1974), 259.

7. Joseph C. Rost, *Leadership for the Twenty-First Century* (Westport, CT: Praeger Publishers, 1993), 44.

8. Peter Drucker, *Leader of the Future* (San Francisco: Jossey-Bass, 1996), xii.

9. John Maxwell, "Leadership Is Influence: Nothing More, Nothing Less," *Christianity Today,* 2005, *http://www.buildingchurchleaders.com/articles/2005/090905.html.*

10. Peter Northouse, *Leadership: Theory and Practice* (Thousand Oaks, CA: Sage, 2010), 3.

11. Rosabeth Moss Kanter, "The Professor as Business Leader," *Ivey Business Journal,* March/April 2006, *http://www.iveybusinessjournal.com/topics/the-workplace/in-conversation-rosabeth-moss-kanter#.*

12. Filomina Chioma Steady, *Women and Leadership in West Africa: Mothering the Nation and Humanizing the State* (New York: Palgrave Macmillan, 2011), 218.

13. Martha Zurita, *Development of Latino Leadership* (South Bend, IN: Univ. of Notre Dame, 2005), 1, *http://latinostudies.nd.edu/assets /95259/original/cct_lo2.pdf.*

14. Northouse, *Leadership*, 2–3.

15. Henry Blackaby and Richard Blackaby, *Spiritual Leadership* (Nashville: Broadman and Holman, 2001), 9.

16. George Barna, *Leaders on Leadership: Wisdom, Advice, and Encouragement on the Art of Leading God's People* (Ventura, CA: Regal, 1997), 24.

17. Ken Blanchard and Phil Hodges, *Lead Like Jesus: Lessons from the Greatest Leadership Role Model of All Time* (Nashville: Thomas Nelson, 2005), 5.

18. Robert Clinton, *The Making of a Leader* (Colorado Springs: NavPress, 1988), 203.

19. Greg Ogden and Daniel Meyer, *Leadership Essentials: Shaping Vision, Multiplying Influence, Defining Character* (Downers Grove, IL: InterVarsity, 2007), 9.

20. Blackaby and Blackaby, *Spiritual Leadership*, 20.

21. Timothy Laniak, *Shepherds After My Own Heart: Pastoral Traditions and Leadership in the Bible* (Downers Grove, IL: InterVarsity, 2006), 57.

22. Ibid., 54.

23. Ibid., 247.

24. Daniel J. Simons and Melinda S. Jensen, "The Effects of Individual Difference and Task Difficulty on Inattentional Blindness," *Psychonomic Bulletin and Review* 16, no. 2 (2009): 398–403.

25. The first time I saw the video, I missed the gorilla, which is all the more embarrassing because I knew the video was about inattentional blindness!

26. T. M. Buescher, P. Olszewski, and S. J. Higham, *Influences on Strategies Adolescents Use to Cope with Their Own Recognized Talents* (Report No. EC 200 755). Paper presented at the biennial meeting of the Society for Research in Child Development, Baltimore, Maryland (1987).

27. Ken Schroeder, "Gifted Girls Hiding," *Education Digest* 62 (December 1996).

CHAPTER 3: THE INVISIBLE ARMY

1. Scot McKnight, *Junia Is Not Alone* (Englewood, CO: Patheos Press, 2011), Kindle edition.

2. I know firsthand how complicated numbers are. In college, I would have flunked algebra had I not dropped it first. When I finally took the class again years later, I had to go to tutorial every single day for a year to get through it. But, trust me, the numbers in this chapter are nowhere near as difficult as figuring out the solution to $x + 9 = 18 - 2x$ (hint: $x = 3$).

3. Michael Margolis, *Believe Me: Why Your Vision, Brand, and Leadership Need a Bigger Story* (New York: Get Started Press, 2009), xv.

4. Matthew Henry and Thomas Scott, *A Commentary on the Holy Bible: From Joshua to Esther* (London: Religious Tract Society, 1895), 11.

5. Mimi Barnard, "Women in the Halls," *Council for Christian Colleges and Universities*, July 2011, *http://www.cccu.org/professional_development/women_in_the_halls_july_2011*.

6. Annual data tables reveal that despite more schools reporting enrollment, the number of students enrolled in these organizations of higher learning has decreased (*http://www.ats.edu/resources/institutional-data/annual-data-tables*).

7. The Association of Theological Schools, "Fact Book on Theological Education 2006–2007" (Pittsburgh: Association of

Theological Schools, 2007), *http://www.ats.edu/resources/institutional-data/annual-data-tables*.

8. Barna Group, "Number of Female Senior Pastors in Protestant Churches Doubles in Past Decade," September 14, 2009, *http://www.barna.org/barna-update/article/17-leadership/304-number-of-female-senior-pastors-in-protestant-churches-doubles-in-past-decade*.

9. Faith Communities Today, "Overall Findings," *http://faithcommunitiestoday.org/fact-2010*.

10. Ibid.

CHAPTER 4: CALLING

1. Mihaly Csikszentmihalyi, *Flow: The Psychology of Optimal Experience* (New York: HarperCollins, 2008), 4.

2. Gene Edward Veith, *God at Work* (Wheaton, IL: Crossway, 2002), 19.

3. Martin Luther, Henry Eyster Jacobs, and Adolph Spaeth, *Works of Martin Luther, with Introductions and Notes* (Philadelphia: A. J. Holman, 1915), Google Books, (accessed March 1, 2013).

4. Veith, *God at Work*, 19.

5. Richard Robert Osmer, *The Teaching Ministry of Congregations* (Louisville: Westminster John Knox, 2005), 177.

6. Oscar Wilde, *The Selfish Giant* (New York: Putnam and Grosser, 1995).

7. Sharon Jayson, "What's on Americans' Minds? Increasingly, 'Me,'" *USA Today*, July 10, 2012, *http://usatoday30.usatoday.com/news/health/story/2012-07-10/individualist-language-in-books/56134152/1*.

8. Parker Palmer, *Let Your Life Speak* (San Francisco: Jossey-Bass, 1999), 10.

9. In the final three paragraphs of his book, Palmer briefly references the communal aspect of calling, but even here the importance of community is vague.

10. Veith, *God at Work*, 21.

11. The others are Romans 12:3−8 and 1 Corinthians 12.

12. Craig Keener, *The IVP Bible Background Commentary* (Downers Grove, IL: InterVarsity, 1994), 334.

13. Augustine, *Confessions* (New York: Oxford Univ. Press, 2008), 3.

14. Walter Elwell, ed., *Evangelical Dictionary of Theology*, 2nd ed. (Grand Rapids, MI: Baker Academic, 2001), 1135.

15. Miroslav Volf, *Work in the Spirit: Toward a Theology of Work* (Eugene, OR: Wipf and Stock, 1991), 112.

16. Frederick Buechner, *Whistling in the Dark* (San Francisco: HarperOne, 1993), 117.

CHAPTER 5: GREAT EXPECTATIONS

1. Marcus Buckingham, "What's Happening to Women's Happiness?" *Huffington Post*, September 17, 2009, *http://www.huffington post.com/marcus-buckingham/whats-happening-to-womens_b_289511 .html*.

2. Betsy Stevenson and Justin Wolfers, "The Paradox of Declining Female Happiness," NBER Working Paper Series (Cambridge, MA: National Bureau of Economic Research, 2009).

3. Barna Group, "Christian Women Today: A Look at Women's Lifestyles, Priorities, and Time Commitments," August 17, 2012, *https://www.barna.org/culture-articles/585-christian-women-today-part-2-of-4-a-look-at-womens-lifestyles-priorities-and-time-commitments* (accessed January 14, 2013).

4. Ibid.

5. Kate Fox, "Mirror, Mirror: A Summary of Research Findings on Body Image," Social Issues Research Centre, 1997, *http://www .sirc.org/publik/mirror.html*.

6. Sharon Hayes and Stacey Tantleff-Dunn, "Am I Too Fat to Be a Princess? Examining the Effects of Popular Media on Young

Girls' Body Image," *British Journal of Developmental Psychology* 48, no. 2 (2010): 413–26.

7. American Time Use Survey, *http://www.bls.gov/tus/*.

8. Barna Group, "Christian Women Today."

9. Ibid.

10. Catalyst, "Breadwinner Moms: Mothers Are the Sole or Primary Provider in Four-in-Ten Households with Children," *http://www .pewsocialtrends.org/2013/05/29/breadwinner-moms/* (accessed June 5, 2013).

11. Augustine, *St. Augustine Prayer Book*.

12. Rebecca Konyndyk DeYoung, *Glittering Vices: A New Look at the Seven Deadly Sins and Their Vices* (Grand Rapids, MI: Brazos, 2009).

CHAPTER 6: IRON LADIES

1. Shawna Lafreniere.

2. Barbara Kellerman and Deborah Rhode, *Women and Leadership: State of Play and Strategies for Change* (San Francisco: Jossey-Bass, 2007).

3. Jessica Stark, "Recommendation Letters May Be Costing Women Jobs, Promotions," *Rice University News and Media*, *http:// news.rice.edu/2010/11/09/recommendation-letters-may-be-costing-women-jobs-promotions-2/*.

4. An example is Sally Helgesen, *The Female Advantage: Women's Ways of Leadership* (New York: Doubleday Currency, 1995).

5. Alice Eagly and Steven Karau, "Role Congruity Theory of Prejudice," *Psychological Review* 109, no. 3 (July 2002): 573–98.

6. Sarah Sumner, *Men and Women in the Church: Building Consensus about Christian Leadership* (Downers Grove, IL: InterVarsity, 2003).

CHAPTER 7: SUPERWOMEN

1. Corrie ten Boom, *The Hiding Place* (1974; Grand Rapids, MI: Chosen, 2006).

2. Ellen McGirt, "Meet the League of Extraordinary Women: Sixty Influencers Who Are Changing the World," *Fast Company*, June 18, 2012.

3. Susan Eisenberger, *We'll Call You If We Need You: Experiences of Women Working Construction* (Ithaca, NY: Cornell Univ. Press, 1998), 4.

4. Gordon Fee, *The First Epistle to the Corinthians* (Grand Rapids, MI: Eerdmans, 1987), 172.

5. A. W. Tozer, *The Knowledge of the Holy* (1961; New York: Harper Collins, 2009), 1.

6. Fyodor Dostoevsky, *The Brothers Karamazov* (New York: Farrar, Straus and Giroux, 1990), 26.

7. Julie Zeilinger, "Why Millennial Women Do Not Want to Lead," *Forbes*, July 16, 2012, *http://www.forbes.com/sites/deniserestauri/2012/07/16/why-millennial-women-do-not-want-to-lead/*.

8. Courtney Martin, *Perfect Girls, Starving Daughters* (New York: Free Press, 2007), 45.

9. Millard Erickson, *Christian Theology* (Grand Rapids, MI: Baker Academic, 1998).

10. Wayne Grudem, *Systematic Theology: An Introduction to Biblical Doctrine* (Grand Rapids, MI: Zondervan), 1994.

11. Gordon Lewis and Bruce Demarest, *Integrative Theology* (Grand Rapids, MI: Zondervan, 1996).

12. J. Scott Duvall and J. Daniel Hayes, *Grasping God's Word: A Hands-On Approach to Reading, Interpreting, and Applying the Bible* (Grand Rapids, MI: Zondervan, 2012).

13. Michael Anthony, *Foundations of Ministry: An Introduction to Christian Education for a New Generation* (Grand Rapids, MI: Baker Academic, 1998).

14. C. S. Lewis, *The Great Divorce* (New York: HarperCollins, 2001), 118.

CHAPTER 8: BRAVE NEW WOMEN

1. Carolyn Custis James, *Half the Church: Recapturing God's Global Vision for Women* (Grand Rapids, MI: Zondervan, 2011), 19.

2. Alexis de Tocqueville, *Democracy in America*, vol. 1 (Stilwell, KS: Digireads.com), 23.

3. Patricia Chapman, "Women's Ministry," in *Evangelical Dictionary of Christian Education*, ed. Michael Anthony (Grand Rapids, MI: Baker, 2001), 725–27.

4. Amy Carmichael, *Kohila: The Shaping of an Indian Nurse*, reprint (Fort Washington, PA: CLC Books, 2002), 166.

5. George Barna, "Twenty Years of Surveys Show Key Differences in the Faith of America's Men and Women," August 1, 2011, *https://www.barna.org/barna-update/faith-spirituality/508-20-years-of-surveys-show-key-differences-in-the-faith-of-americas-men-and-women#.*

6. Elisabeth Kelan, *Rising Stars: Developing Millennial Women as Leaders* (Houndmills, Basingstoke, Hampshire, UK: Palgrave Macmillan, 2012), 56.

7. T. A. Kenner, *Symbols and Their Hidden Meanings* (New York: Thunder's Mouth Press, 2006), 7.

8. *The Breakfast Club*, directed by John Hughes (NBC Universal, 1985), film.

9. Jean Twenge, "A Review of the Empirical Evidence on Generational Differences in Work Attitudes," *Journal of Business and Psychology* 25, no. 2 (2010).

10. Alan Hirsch, *The Forgotten Ways* (Grand Rapids, MI: Brazos, 2006), 221.

11. Antoine de Saint-Exupery, *Wind, Sand, and Stars* (Orlando: Harcourt, 2002), 215.

12. Hirsch, *Forgotten Ways*, 220.

13. Victor Turner, *The Ritual Process: Structure and Anti-Structure* (New York: Aldine de Gruyter, 1939), 107.

14. Hirsch, *Forgotten Ways*, 221.

CHAPTER 9: LOCKED DOORS AND DETOURS

1. Gladys Aylward, *The Little Woman* (Chicago: Moody, 1970), 8.

2. Alan Burgess, *The Small Woman* (Cutchogue, NY: Buccaneer Books, 1996), 18.

3. Aylward, *Little Woman*, 9.

4. Foot-binding is the practice of wrapping the feet of young girls, and in some cases breaking the bones in the feet, to achieve the prized shape of a "three-inch golden lotus." The entire foot would be wrapped with a bandage, pulling the toes in toward the heel. Foot-binding caused constant, immense pain, but was considered crucial to obtaining a marriage proposal. For a deep treatment of the issue, see Wang Ping's *Aching for Beauty: Foot-binding in China.*

5. Aylward, *Little Woman*, 153.

6. Alice H. Eagly and Linda Carli, *Through the Labyrinth: The Truth about How Women Become Leaders* (Boston: Harvard Business School Publishing, 2007), 6.

7. Ibid.

8. The Barna Group, "Are Women Happy at Church?" August 14, 2012, *https://www.barna.org/culture-articles/579-christian-women-today-part1-of-4-what-women-think-of-faith-leadership-and-their-role-in-the-church.*

9. Jim Henderson, *Resignation of Eve* (Carol Stream, IL: Barna-Books, 2012), 165–66.

10. George Barna, "Twenty Years of Surveys Show Key Differences in the Faith of America's Men and Women," August 1, 2011, *https://www.barna.org/barna-update/faith-spirituality/508-20*

-years-of-surveys-show-key-differences-in-the-faith-of-americas-men -and-women#.

11. Simone de Beauvoir, *The Second Sex*, quoted in Ruth A. Tucker and Walter L. Liefeld, *Daughters of the Church* (Grand Rapids, MI: Zondervan, 1987), 403.

12. Elisa Morgan, *She Did What She Could: Five Words of Jesus That Will Change Your Life* (Carol Stream, IL: Tyndale, 2009).

13. Mother Teresa, *Come Be My Light: The Private Writings of the Saint of Calcutta* (New York: Random House, 2009), 34.

14. Ibid.

15. *Aesop's Fables*, trans. Vernon Jones (New York: Barnes and Noble, 2003), 52.

CHAPTER 10: LET'S TALK ABOUT SEX

1. Catalyst, "Women and Men in U.S. Corporate Leadership: Same Workplace, Different Realities?" June 15, 2004, *http://www.wallnetwork.ca/inequity/3cat_corporatelead.pdf*.

2. *Merriam Webster Online Dictionary*, s.v. "platonic," *www.merriam-webster.com/dictionary/platonic* (accessed February 16, 2012).

3. Georgia Harness, *Women in Church and Society* (New York: Abingdon, 1972), 54.

4. Sun Tzu, *The Art of War* (Blacksburg, VA: Thrifty Books, 2009), 17.

5. John T. Bristow, *What Paul Really Said about Women* (New York: HarperCollins, 1991), 4.

6. Sarah B. Pomeroy, *Goddesses, Whores, Wives, and Slaves* (New York: Random House, 1995), 122.

7. Although some may argue that the New Testament presents women as socially inferior to men, the emphasis here is on the perceived ontological inferiority of women, which is not found in the New Testament. Therefore, I left the New Testament out of the discussion here.

8. A big thank you to Kevan Gray, my dad, for figuring this complex calculation for me!

9. C. S. Lewis, *The Four Loves* (Orlando: Harcourt Brace, 1988), 87.

10. Ibid., 88.

11. Ibid., 87.

12. Gail Collins, *America's Women* (New York: HarperCollins, 2003), 449.

13. April Bleske-Rechek, et al. "Benefit or Burden: Attraction in Cross-Sex Friendship," *Journal of Social and Personal Relationships* 29, no. 5: 569–96.

14. Ibid.

15. Anne Cronin, "Between Friends: Making Emotions Intersubjectively," *Emotion, Space and Society* (2013).

16. Laurence Gonzales, *Deep Survival: Who Lives, Who Dies, and Why* (New York: Norton, 2003), 133.

17. Sue Edwards and Kelley Matthews, *Mixed Ministry: Working Together as Brothers and Sisters in an Oversexed Society* (Grand Rapids, MI: Kregel, 2008), 174.

18. Catalyst, "Mentoring: Necessary but Insufficient for Advancement," December 1, 2010, *http://www.catalyst.org/uploads/mentoring necessarybutinsufficientforadvancement.pdf* (accessed June 12, 2013).

19. Father Cantalamessa, "Francis and Clare: In Love, but with Whom?" October 4, 2007, *http://www.zenit.org/en/articles/francis-and-clare-in-love-but-with-whom* (accessed February 29, 2013).

CHAPTER 11: THE AUDACITY OF COURAGE

1. Henryk Sienkiewicz, *Quo Vadis* (Charleston, SC: Createspace, 2011), 393–94.

2. Craig Keener, *The Gospel of Matthew: A Socio-Rhetorical Commentary* (Grand Rapids, MI: Eerdmans, 2009), 637.

3. C. S. Lewis, *The Screwtape Letters* (New York: HarperCollins, 1996), 161.

4. Paul Tillich, *The Courage to Be* (New Haven, CT: Yale Univ. Press, 2000), 7.

5. There are, of course, many more internal struggles than fear, bitterness, and burnout, such as depression, insecurity, and anxiety, but I tackle these three because I think much of what we struggle with is rooted in these three primary problems.

6. While fear and anxiety are experienced the same way, fear is a response to a known, specific danger while anxiety is a vague feeling or worry or nervousness about an unknown, unspecific danger.

7. Michael Linden and Andreas Maercker, *Embitterment: Societal, Psychological, and Clinical Perspectives* (Germany: Springer-Verlag Wien, 2011), 10.

8. In Deuteronomy 29:18, Israel is instructed to "beware lest there be among you a root bearing poisonous and bitter fruit" and in Hebrews 12:15 to "see to it ... that no 'root of bitterness' springs up and causes trouble, and by it many become defiled."

9. Richard Swenson, *Margin: Restoring Emotional, Physical, Financial, and Time Reserves to Overloaded Lives* (Colorado Springs, CO: NavPress, 2004), 93.

10. Acts of St. Peter, *The Apocryphal New Testament, M. R. James Translation and Notes* (Oxford: Clarendon Press, 1924), *http://www.earlychristianwritings.com/text/actspeter.html* (accessed March 3, 2013).

11. Ibid.

CHAPTER 12: LIVE WELL, LOVE WELL, LEAD WELL

1. Grover Levy, "If You Want to Lead Me to Jesus," Word Records, Word Entertainment Media, December 18, 2007.

2. Ibid.

3. Alexandre Havard, *The Virtuous Leader: An Agenda for Personal Excellence* (New Rochelle, NY: Scepter, 2007), xiii.

4. Warren Bennis, Daniel Goleman, James O'Toole, and Patricia Ward Biederman, *Transparency: Creating a Culture of Candor* (San Francisco: Jossey-Bass, 2008), 3.

5. It is far too easy for pastors to hop from church to church without accurate and complete background checks to ensure that they have been living with integrity or have received appropriate treatment and accountability if they have not.

6. Aleksandr Solzhenitsyn, *The Gulag Archipelago 1918–1956: An Experiment in Literary Investigation*, vol. 1 (Boulder, CO: Westview, 1998), 178.

7. J. P. Moreland and Klaus Issler, *The Lost Virtue of Happiness* (Colorado Springs: NavPress, 2006), 25.

8. Pope Benedict XVI, *The Virtues* (Huntington, IN: Our Sunday Visitor Publishing Division, 2010), 15.

9. Ibid.

10. James Keenan, *Moral Wisdom: Lessons and Texts from the Catholic Tradition* (Lanham, MD: Rowman and Littlefield, 2010), 158.

11. Pope Benedict XVI, *The Virtues*, 16.

12. Saint Thomas Aquinas, *The Cardinal Virtues: Prudence, Justice, Fortitude, and Temperance*, reprint (Indianapolis: Hackett, 2005), 163.

13. Ibid., 1.

14. Havard, *Virtuous Leader*, 68.

15. Aquinas, *Cardinal Virtues*, 161.

16. Michael Slote, "Justice as a Virtue," *Stanford Encyclopedia of Philosophy*, Fall 2010 edition, ed. Edward N. Zalta, *http://plato.stanford.edu/archives/fall2010/entries/justice-virtue/*.

17. Aquinas, *Cardinal Virtues*, 164.

18. Havard, *Virtuous Leader*, 85.

19. Aquinas, *Cardinal Virtues*, 159.

20. Havard, *Virtuous Leader*, xviii.

21. Ibid., 4.

22. I highly recommend Adele Calhoun's *Spiritual Disciplines Handbook: Practices That Transform Us* (Downers Grove, IL: InterVarsity, 2005).

23. Calhoun, *Spiritual Disciplines Handbook*, 12.